Just Ask Wim!

Down-to-Earth Gardening Answers

Just Ask Wim!

Down-to-Earth Gardening Answers

Wim Vander Zalm

Perry,

May your green thumb
get greener ♡
Grow, Enjoy, Flourish!

HARBOUR
PUBLISHING

ACKNOWLEDGEMENTS

It takes a village to write a book…

Over the years, I've learned so much through talking to friends, family and my customers, who have all in some way made me feel it was necessary to keep educating myself in the world of gardening. Unlike running into a medical doctor at the grocery store, no one is ever afraid of asking questions of a plant doctor in any social setting: garden questions don't require showing any body parts. So thanks to everyone for their questions—if I didn't have the answer, I would research it until I did.

Relating to this book I would like to thank:

Jay Shaw of Jay Shaw Photography for many spectacular photographs throughout this book, and for doing his best to make photos of me look good. Thanks, Jay, we tried!

Shelagh Themmen for proofing and verifying all Latin names, species or any really complicated words. Just joking. Ensuring the exact spelling of many, many plant names can be very time-consuming, so thank you, Shelagh, for your patience.

Carol Pope for convincing me to write this book by assuring me that it wouldn't take too much of my time. I might dispute that one a bit. Thank you, Carol, for keeping me focused and inspired. There are so many parts, pieces and much crafting required as a book evolves, and your experience and knowledge was an incredible asset to this project.

Sincere thanks, too, to this book's designer, Roger Handling, and to the whole Harbour Publishing team.

Truly, there are many people who have played an important role in some way in the making of this book and I have appreciated everyone's input. To all of those who have been part of this journey, thank you.

Wim

CONTENTS

*Previous spread: The lovely pom pom dahlia
can be enjoyed in the garden but also makes a
long-lasting cut flower. NFBIC photo*

Preface

Q.

What vegetables can I plant as winter crops? How can I avoid bitter bolting lettuce? When is the best time to cut back rhodos? How do I overwinter my geraniums and fuchsias? What fast-growing evergreen hedge will work for my narrow urban yard? How late can I plant spring-flowering bulbs? What should I do about the chafer infestation that is destroying my lawn? Why aren't my berries bigger? Which fruits and vegetables grow best in patio pots? What's the best way to grow basil? How can I build a quick and easy vertical herb garden?

These are just a few of the 100 + burning questions that renowned garden expert Wim Vander Zalm has answered again and again as owner of two garden centres for nearly three decades and a long-time regular on *The Bill Good Show*. Wim is also a frequent guest on *Studio 4 with Fanny Kiefer* on Shaw Cable TV, the host for 15 years of CKNW's *Garden Talk* program and the Q&A columnist for a decade for *GardenWise* and *BC Home & Garden* magazines. He is known to many as the "plant doctor" who has gardeners everywhere turning to his website to "Ask Wim."

Certainly, if it's a garden query, Wim has answered it. And if it's a plant quandary, he has put his finger on it for customers who have brought him botanical samples by the bucket-load year after year. In this book, Wim covers all the horticultural hot spots: vegetables, fruit and berries, herbs, annuals and perennials, patio and container gardens, shrubs, trees, hedges and vines, plus how to grow a healthy lawn organically—or not, as the top turf-replacing groundcovers are yet another topic. Wim also includes organic pest and weed management, common-sense pruning tips, and fertilization and soil-building advice alongside the much-loved mulch recipes his radio listeners ask him to repeat every spring and fall.

Friendly, often funny and always down to earth, Wim is the guy to ask whenever there is a need to know how to make the most of any garden—urban or otherwise. In addition, his "most comprehensive ever" checklist takes the reader right through the year, month by month, and pinpoints just what to do and when for a stress-free, successful and super-satisfying gardening experience.

Carol Pope, *Garden Editor*

Introduction

I've often wondered where my love for gardening began. Although it may have been inherent, or learned by osmosis—as our family has a long history in horticulture—it could also be because of a game I traditionally played whenever I was in the car with my dad. I would repeatedly ask him to name plants that I pointed to in the gardens we passed, scrambling to find the next plant that just might stump him. Without a doubt, that silly occupation made me more observant of my surroundings year in and year out, giving me cause to evaluate how, why and when plants bloomed, yellowed, grew leaves, dropped leaves, were pruned and so much more. I was quietly being schooled about the horticultural world around me.

The passion grew and by age 13, with the help of Cam, a school buddy, I built a 200-square-foot greenhouse in my parents' backyard. What type of nerd does that at age 13? Still, I found it very rewarding, both mentally and financially, taking cuttings and propagating different types of plants, which I sold at my dad's garden centre.

However, I can't say that I enjoyed all aspects of gardening as a young

Growing fruit trees is what we do here in British Columbia. This book will help you get your orchard started!

Jay Shaw photo

Introduction

man. Although our family was fortunate enough to have a ride-on lawn mower, there were still four acres of lawn that needed to be cut...and putting that mower into overdrive was not beneficial to a couple of young fruit trees that simply appeared out of nowhere.

At age 19, I was in charge of one of the largest garden centres in the province, and it was from this point forward that I learned the most—more specifically, from my customers. Every gardening question has a story behind it, and I gleaned endless details about the ailing plant's journey and other particulars that in turn enlarged my horticultural knowledge.

When Carol Pope, my editor, encouraged me to write a book, I began to have a closer look at other gardening volumes. Although there are some spectacular examples, most seem to be written for those who already know a lot about gardening. Personally, if I wanted to learn about car engines, I wouldn't be looking for technical talk, because I truly know nothing about them.

Through many years of answering gardening questions on my radio show and on TV—or through inspecting a myriad of plastic baggies with samples of bugs, leaves or fungus brought to me by my customers—I have learned that most people want enough information to solve a problem but not the kind of technical language that makes their eyes start to glaze over.

This book will answer more than 100 of the most-asked gardening questions—with solid, common-sense answers. And from each Q&A, you'll learn the how and why that will, without a doubt, make *you* a better gardener.

Wim

Wim's Month-by-Month Garden Checklist

Wim's Month-by-Month Garden Checklist

There always seems to be too much to do, both inside and outside the home, and sometimes it just makes it easier to break it down into smaller blocks of time—months, for example—so that we don't feel so overwhelmed. This comprehensive checklist takes you through the year on a month-by-month basis, with what to do and *when*—and just about everything you need to tick off to make your garden the best it can be:

JANUARY

- ☐ In regions where the ground is not frozen or too wet, dig over vacant vegetable plots not turned already.

- ☐ Inspect stored tubers and bulbs (dahlia, begonias, cannas, etc.) for rot or dehydration (see page 102).

- ☐ Prune apple, pear and plum trees (see page 200).

- ☐ Prune blueberry plants (see page 201).

- ☐ Prune grapevines.

- ☐ Add 22 1b. (10 kg) manure around rhubarb.

- ☐ Plan your vegetable crop rotation for the coming season.

Pear trees are easy to grow and bear delicious fruit, but remember to prune them in the winter!

Remember the birds: this time of year, they need seed, high-energy suet and water. ☐

Water outdoor perennials or shrub containers not exposed to rain. ☐

Recycle your Christmas tree: cut up the small branches for the compost and plan to use the trunk as a pole for beans or other climbing crops. ☐

Turn the ingredients in your compost box (see page 237). ☐

Stay off your lawn as much as possible during frost periods. ☐

Sow geranium and impatiens seeds inside. ☐

FEBRUARY

Prepare vegetable seedbeds and sow some cold-tolerant vegetables indoors in a bright, warm spot for planting outdoors after they've grown to at least 2 in. (5 cm). You'll have to acclimatize them for the outdoors and protect them from freezing temperatures for the first few weeks (see page 40). ☐

Prune winter-flowering shrubs that have finished blooming (see page 198). ☐

Complete your second winter application of lime sulphur and dormant oil spray (dormant spray) on deciduous trees and shrubs to kill overwintering fungus diseases and insects (see page 215). ☐

Winter-prune your wisteria (see page 202). ☐

Prune hardy evergreen hedges to tidy them up. ☐

Cut back hardy deciduous hedges to desired height (see page 200). ☐

Cut back ornamental grasses to the ground. ☐

Lime the lawn and garden (see page 173), avoiding acid-loving plants (see page 115). ☐

Water outdoor perennials or shrubs in containers that are not exposed to rain. ☐

Cut the blooms off of your poinsettia (see page 90). ☐

Start begonia tubers indoors. ☐

Poinsettias are festive and can survive year round with a little care. That is, if you want a poinsettia around all year.

☐ Service your lawn mower.

☐ Move winter-stored geraniums and fuchsias to a cool, bright location and prune back to mature stems (see page 78).

☐ Mix manure into your vegetable garden (see page 35).

☐ Sow cole-crop seeds indoors (see page 40).

☐ Did you receive flowers for Valentine's Day? Make two fresh cuts a week, taking off 1 in. (2.5 cm) of the stem, to help them last longer.

☐ Select your crops for the year by organizing your seeds collection and purchasing fresh seeds from your local garden centre.

☐ Turn the ingredients in your compost box (see page 237).

☐ Remove any remaining leaves from your rose bushes and collect fallen leaves below them to ensure any black-spot infections from the previous year won't infect this season's growth. Do not compost the leaves if there are any signs of disease.

☐ Prune summer-flowering clematis.

Apply the first application of lime around your lilac (see page 126). ☐

Feed hedging cedars with a slow-release high-nitrogen fertilizer. ☐

MARCH

Plant shallots, onion sets and early potatoes. ☐

Protect new spring perennial shoots from slugs (see page 220). ☐

Shear winter-blooming heather, now that it's finished flowering. ☐

Plant summer-flowering bulbs (see page 79). ☐

Plant new berry crops (see page 51). ☐

Lift and divide overgrown clumps of perennials (see page 106). ☐

Top-dress and mix fresh compost into your patio containers (see page 143). ☐

Mow the lawn on dry days (if needed). ☐

Aerate your lawn (see page 172). ☐

Weeds are starting to grow; deal with them before they get out of hand (see page 228). ☐

Perennials like this candytuft, need to be protected from slugs and divided (if overgrown) in March.

☐ Start feeding fish in water features.

☐ Prune forsythia when it has finished blooming.

☐ Prune your rose bushes (see page 204).

☐ Feed your spring-blooming bulbs after they have finished blooming (see page 99).

☐ Prune your perennial herbs (see page 65).

☐ Looking for a specific rose? Selection is at its best at your local garden centre now, and it's a great time to plant them.

☐ Watch for manure sales from garden centres and club fundraisers and stock up.

☐ Feed your lawn with a spring-formulation fertilizer (see page 175).

☐ Apply lime to hydrangea to keep them pink, or use aluminum sulphate to keep them blue (see page 243).

☐ Eradicate dandelions from your lawn using a quick trick (see page 178).

☐ March is a great month for transplanting trees and shrubs (see page 188).

☐ Mulch rows of raspberries with a 4-in. (10-cm) layer of compost or manure (see page 55).

☐ Ensure peony rings or other support systems are placed around plants before they reach 6 in. (15 cm) in height.

☐ Start feeding houseplants on a monthly basis.

☐ Sow leafy vegetables indoors for planting outdoors in April (see page 40).

☐ Expand your perennial and groundcover selection in your yard by planting them now; selection is at its best at your local garden centre in March and April.

☐ Plant fruit trees now; selection is at its best at your local garden centre this month.

☐ Treat your fruit trees and bushes, rose bushes and any other deciduous trees and shrubs with lime sulphur and dormant oil spray prior to buds opening (see page 215).

Purchase and plant summer- and fall-flowering bulbs now, while the selection is at its best. ☐

Start feeding your trees, shrubs, perennials and vines with appropriate organic fertilizer. ☐

Deadhead all of your spring-blooming bulbs, such as tulips, daffodils and hyacinths, after the flowers have finished—but not until the foliage has died back (see page 103). ☐

Direct-sow peas and beans and secure netting or poles for support. ☐

Divide perennials. ☐

Prune rose bushes (see page 204). ☐

Power-rake your lawn (see page 180). ☐

If you have an in-ground irrigation system, check each sprinkler head to ensure it's working and properly directed. ☐

Plant perennial herbs (see page 64). ☐

Ensure the drain holes in your garden pots are not plugged (see page 142). ☐

Empty one-third of the compost box from its base for mixing into your garden and planters. ☐

Herb selections are best in spring with new varieties appearing each year. Prune in March for the best results.

APRIL

☐ Continue to keep weeds in check.

☐ Guide and tie climbing roses.

☐ Sow annual flower seeds and herb seeds.

☐ Start to increase the watering frequency, with the addition of fertilizer at half strength, for any overwintered plants, such as citrus, bougainvillea and datura.

☐ Increase the frequency of your houseplant watering.

☐ Feed deciduous shrubs.

☐ Sow new lawns or repair bare spots (see page 166).

☐ Prune your fig tree.

☐ Divide bamboo plants.

☐ Prune back houseplants if required.

☐ Bring out your stored dahlias, gladiolas and cannas, and discard any bulbs, roots or tubers that have dehydrated or rotted. Plant the healthy ones outdoors (see page 102).

☐ Plant your summer-blooming hanging baskets (see page 138).

☐ Start feeding hanging baskets every two weeks right through August.

☐ Prune rhododendrons (see page 206) and azaleas (see page 205) after they have finished blooming.

☐ Remove slugs from the tender new shoots of your perennials.

☐ Sow tomato seeds inside.

☐ Repot houseplants if they appear to be rootbound.

☐ Divide perennials where necessary (see page 108).

☐ Control moss in your lawn and garden (see page 170).

☐ Scrape excess lichen growth from trees with a wire brush.

Top-dress and overseed your lawn (see page 169). ☐

Plant out tomato plants but protect them from cold (see page 37). ☐

Turn the ingredients in your compost box (see page 237). ☐

MAY

Watch the weather forecast and protect plants that could be damaged by frost by covering them with newspaper or white garden fabric. ☐

Harden off patio plants such as hibiscus, bougainvillea and datura by introducing them gradually to the cooler temperatures of the outdoors in preparation for summer. ☐

Regularly pull or hoe out weeds from vegetable and flower gardens before they flower and set seed. ☐

Rock-garden perennial groundcovers, such as aubretia, iberis and alyssum, should be sheared. ☐

Crisp, white tiny flowers cover this aubretia. It is a hardy rockery perennial that shines in early spring. I've enjoyed mine hanging over a rock wall in my yard for nearly 15 years. There's value from a $4 perennial!

☐ Shear back perennial herbs (see page 65).

☐ Plant out summer annuals, unless you live in a colder region.

☐ Collect rainwater, if possible, for watering lawns and gardens.

☐ Mow lawns weekly.

☐ Lift and divide overcrowded clumps of daffodils and other spring-flowering bulbs (see page 104).

☐ Check spruce for spruce aphid and control with organic pyrethrum spray.

☐ Sow new lawns (see page 166).

☐ Place a 6-in. (15-cm) layer of compost and coir (my preference) or peat moss around blueberries.

☐ Layer 2–4 in. (5–10 cm) of mulch (see page 118) around your rhododendrons and azaleas.

☐ Deadhead tulips, daffodils and other bulbs once they have finished blooming.

☐ Place your poinsettia outdoors and cut the plant to half its height.

☐ Place your amaryllis outdoors or even plant it in the garden for the summer (see page 88).

☐ Fertilize your lawn with a slow-release high-nitrogen fertilizer.

☐ Deadhead rhododendrons.

☐ In late May, plant out your soft annual herbs, such as basil and cilantro.

☐ Turn the ingredients in your compost box (see page 237).

JUNE

☐ This is the month where weeds grow very quickly—keep them in check.

☐ Harvest early lettuce and other greens while they're young, as there's lots more on the way.

A herb bed in a sunny site waits for the next growing season's additions. Remember, basil is always the last herb to be planted, as it will not tolerate cold nights.

Harvest radish and early potatoes. ☐

Continue to cut your lawn once a week. ☐

Stake tall and floppy plants, particularly many top-heavy perennials. ☐

Prune spring-flowering shrubs if they have finished blooming. ☐

Shear most hedges. ☐

Inspect plants carefully and regularly for insects over the next three months, as this is when they are most prevalent. ☐

Feed all herbs, fruits and vegetables with compost tea. ☐

Remove suckers from tomato plants (see page 38). ☐

Release ladybugs to control aphids on the plants in your yard. ☐

Stake dahlias, being careful not to spear the tubers. ☐

Shear spring-blooming heather to keep it full. ☐

Sow vegetable seeds to accommodate progressive planting as crops are harvested. ☐

Replace cool-loving spinach crops with heat-loving beans. ☐

☐ Prune broadleaf evergreens that have finished blooming, keeping in mind that you may want to harvest some of those greens in December for decorating outdoor planters.

☐ Prune spent blossoms from annuals and perennials as required.

☐ Turn the ingredients in your compost box (see page 237).

JULY

☐ Check clematis for signs of disease or unusual browning of leaves; if necessary, get a diagnosis from the experts at your local garden centre.

☐ Take particular care to water shallow-rooted plants and street trees through dry spells.

☐ Deadhead bedding plants and repeat-flowering perennials to ensure continuous blooming.

☐ Check all fruit trees for unusual blemishes on the leaves or fruit; if necessary, get a diagnosis from the expert at your local garden centre.

☐ Prune and thin your wisteria.

☐ If required, apply a second application to your lawn of a slow-release high-nitrogen fertilizer.

☐ Remove and compost all remaining leaves from any spring-blooming bulbs.

☐ Deadhead rose bushes and prune back to the first set of five leaves.

☐ Feed all fruiting plants, herbs and vegetables with both manure tea and organic liquid fertilizer.

☐ Take your tropical plants outside and give them a thorough hosing down to clean the leaves of collected dust and oils from the winter months.

☐ Water all berry crops and fruiting trees thoroughly at least once a week, increasing the frequency as the summer heats up.

☐ Shear back hanging baskets (see page 75).

Remove composted material from the compost box and spread around shallow-rooted plants. ☐

Harvest crops frequently and freeze, dry or can as many as possible for the winter. ☐

Get the most from your perennial herbs by harvesting from those that have grown sufficiently. Snip portions no smaller than 6–12 in. (15–30 cm) from each stem so that when they flush out, it is from sturdy wood that has the strength to support an abundance of new growth prior to fall. ☐

AUGUST

The heat takes a toll on planters and hanging baskets—ensure you water and feed regularly. ☐

Deadhead annuals regularly to force continued blossoming. ☐

Harvest herbs regularly to force an additional flush of growth for further harvesting in fall. ☐

Sow seeds of winter vegetables (see page 42). ☐

Smart gardeners use every bit of available growing space, even small areas between buildings. Note the lettuce and other leaf crops tucked into this side garden.

- [ ] Cut raspberry canes that have finished fruiting for the year to the ground level, and remove and compost all the debris.

- [ ] Lift and pot up rooted strawberry runners to expand your inventory.

- [ ] Fertilize fruiting bushes, herbs and vegetables with compost tea (see page 238).

- [ ] Thin the leaves of your tomato plants.

- [ ] Prune stone-crop fruit trees.

- [ ] Increase your number of geraniums and fuchsias for the next year by rooting cuttings now.

- [ ] Mid month, take your amaryllis bulb out of the garden or planter and store for six to eight weeks (see page 88).

- [ ] Thin the leaves of your grapevine, particularly around fruit clusters.

- [ ] Turn the ingredients in your compost box (see page 237).

SEPTEMBER

- [ ] Start reducing frequency of houseplant watering.

- [ ] It's the start of the spring-blooming bulb planting season: begin planning placement of tulips, daffodils, hyacinths and so many more (see page 101).

- [ ] Plant winter vegetable seedlings (see page 42).

- [ ] Plant fall rye or other fall cover crops.

- [ ] Feed your lawn and garden with a fall-formulated fertilizer.

- [ ] Sow grass seed to fill in bare, brown or thin lawn areas.

- [ ] Bring your poinsettia indoors and start providing it with long nights by placing it in a dark closet for 16-hour periods for 6 to 8 weeks to colour up the bracts (more commonly referred to as the flower) (see page 90).

- [ ] Reapply lime to your hydrangea to keep it pink, or add aluminum sulphate to keep it blue (see page 243).

Fall mums are a must-have for decorating the front porch. They bloom for long periods and come in an array of colours.

Plant winter pansies, fall mums, fall asters and other late-flowering plants for a splash of autumn colour. ☐

Plant fall-flowering crocus (colchicum). ☐

Get the most from your perennial herbs by harvesting from those that have grown sufficiently. Snip portions no smaller than 6–12 in. (15–30 cm) from each stem so that when they flush out, it is from sturdy wood that has the strength to support an abundance of new growth. ☐

Prior to bringing them inside again, thoroughly wash your tropical plants with a spray nozzle to blast away any insects or insect eggs (see page 215). ☐

Turn the ingredients in your compost box (see page 237). ☐

OCTOBER

Clean up and compost autumn fallen leaves regularly. ☐

Cut back perennials that have died down. ☐

Divide herbaceous perennials and rhubarb (see page 106). ☐

Move tender plants into their protected winter resting area. ☐

October is a great month to plant trees and shrubs (see page 113). ☐

- [ ] Harvest any remaining crops that will be destroyed by frost (see page 41).
- [ ] Harvest all remaining apples, pears, grapes and nuts.
- [ ] Prune climbing, hybrid tea, floribunda, grandiflora, David Austin and groundcover roses (see page 204).
- [ ] Last chance to mow the lawn and trim hedges in mild areas.
- [ ] Bring your amaryllis out of storage and plant it into an 8-in. (20-cm) pot (see page 87).
- [ ] Clean up the debris from herbaceous perennials.
- [ ] Shear summer-blooming heather now that it's finished flowering.
- [ ] Gather vegetable leaves/plants that won't overwinter well and freeze them for future soup stock.
- [ ] Stop feeding houseplants.
- [ ] Store begonia, gladiola and dahlia tubers and canna roots after the first frost (see page 84).
- [ ] Clean dead-needle debris out of the inside of cedar hedges to eliminate an environment for overwintering pests and disease (see page 129).
- [ ] Turn off and blow out in-ground irrigation sprinkler lines.
- [ ] Turn the ingredients in your compost box (see page 237).

NOVEMBER

- [ ] Clean up fallen leaves, particularly from lawns, ponds and flower beds.
- [ ] Raise containers onto pot feet to prevent waterlogging over winter.
- [ ] Last chance to plant spring-blooming bulbs (see page 101).
- [ ] Prune rose bushes back by a third to a half (see page 204).
- [ ] Complete your first application of lime sulphur and dormant oil spray on deciduous trees and shrubs to prevent overwintering insects and fungal diseases (see page 215).

Put out bird food to attract winter birds to your yard. ☐

Prune broadleaf evergreens, pines, cedars, holly and juniper, and use those clippings to create festive displays in your outdoor containers. ☐

Consider transplanting shrubs (see page 191). ☐

Mulch root crops if you intend to leave them in the soil (see page 41). ☐

Plant "prepared" hyacinths and narcissus for indoor forcing for colour and fragrance in December and January (see page 86). ☐

Start or continue harvesting winter veggies from your garden (see page 43). ☐

Time to store geraniums, fuchsias and other non-hardy summer bloomers to protect them from winter cold (see page 77). ☐

DECEMBER

Although they can be pruned at other times of the year, December is a great month to trim your maple and birch trees (see page 209). ☐

Prune apple, pear and plum trees. ☐

A fall afternoon spent raking leaves will ensure your lawn stays healthy and will be in good shape in spring.

Wim's Month-by-Month Garden Checklist

- ☐ Prune broadleaf evergreens, pines, cedars, holly and juniper, and use those clippings to create festive displays in your outdoor containers.

- ☐ Harvest leeks, kale leaves (but leave the plant for spring growth), cabbage, parsnips and root crops as great additions to winter feasts, soups and stews.

- ☐ Transplant larger trees and shrubs (see page 188).

- ☐ Houseplant watering should be half (with exceptions) what it was during the summer months.

- ☐ Water outdoor perennials or shrub containers not exposed to rain.

- ☐ Wrap poinsettias for the ride home from the store to protect them against cold chills.

- ☐ Check the water level of your Christmas tree daily.

- ☐ If you used a live Christmas tree, transition it to the outdoors immediately after Christmas.

- ☐ If it snows, knock the snow off of cedar hedging, evergreen magnolias or any other shrubs that will hold a snowload and potentially bend branches to the point that they snap off.

- ☐ Remove the flower stalk from your amaryllis after it blooms.

- ☐ Make a list of the vegetables that you want to grow next season.

Ornamental kale is a colourful choice in fall for pots or mixed planters. Enjoy it all winter, as the colour often intensifies with colder temperatures.

New To Gardening

New To Gardening

Previous page:

Start small when adding new flower beds and you won't be overwhelmed. You will learn as you go and gain confidence with each success.

New to gardening? Well, everyone has to start somewhere, and just wait until you do! I believe gardening is one of the most rewarding hobbies possible, with so many side benefits for you and your loved ones—from fresh fruits and berries direct from your backyard to delicious herbs to year-round organic salad greens, even if you just have a container garden on your balcony. Plus, you will be enriched by the joy of fragrant flowering bulbs in the springtime, year-round blossoms and greenery to decorate your home inside and out, and, naturally, the exercise that will provide health benefits all of your life.

In fact, my eldest son has recently discovered the many virtues of gardening and, more specifically, the benefits of growing our own crops—tearing up half the back lawn to plant a vegetable garden. My New Age hippie son! It's all spectacular, though, as he's getting results *and* making mistakes. But because of those mistakes he is becoming a wiser and better gardener…and you've got to start somewhere!

Gardening is easy when you break it down into bits and pieces—or if you take it just one question at a time and make it a fun journey. So enjoy your successes and accept any occasional disappointment as just another learning opportunity on your way to becoming a seasoned veteran.

A summer flowering bed that rewards you right through until late fall. NFBIC photo

HOW TO GET STARTED

I just purchased a new home and it needs some landscaping—where do I start? **Q.**

A. First, I suggest you take some photos of your yard to your local nursery and ask the gardeners on staff how to begin. Most importantly, don't bite off more than you can chew. Start small and choose only one area of your yard to focus on. You won't have a *Better Homes and Gardens* landscape in the first year, but it could happen if you take it a step at a time.

If you would like a vegetable garden, choose a spot with full sun (and read the section on page 34). Again, keep it simple, with a few of your favourites. And, whatever garden you plan for, think "right plant, right place." Sun lovers need a sunny spot, and shade lovers must have shade. It's also very important to ensure the mature height and width of the plant is size appropriate for the space it's going in. I often say that plants are what they're grown in—kind of like the expression "You are what you eat." No matter what you plant, ensure that it is tucked in with a healthy amount of good soil, manure, coir or peat moss, compost and sand dug deep into the planting hole. This almost always ensures lush results.

In addition, make notes in a garden journal. Keep the labels from any plants you purchase and record where they are in your yard. This will benefit you down the road if you need more information about when they should be pruned or what they should be fed—noting the identity of your plants enables your local garden centre to answer any questions you come to have about health or maintenance issues as they grow. Visit with samples of the plant in question.

Your local garden centre is a spectacular resource. If you don't know what some of the plants in your yard are, take photos or small cuttings to the garden centre for identification. Don't be shy about doing this—for all the samples I've seen over the years, I should have bought shares in Ziploc! With a bit of information it won't be long before looking after all the plants in your garden simply becomes second nature to you.

TOOLS

Q. *I'm a beginner gardener— what tools do I really need?*

A. **Must-have tools**

The ultimate would be a neighbour who has every gardening tool and is more than happy to lend them to you! But assuming that's not the case, acquiring some tools is as appropriate for the gardener as it is for the mechanic, with every task being that much easier when you have the right equipment.

A good-quality pair of hand pruners is a must. Use these for light pruning and shaping. Blades can be sharpened and replacement springs are available so that you can keep these pruners for years.

I probably have 25 tools in my shed, but I would really like to know how I ended up with 6 shovels. Still, I do have a base of equipment that I depend on, so I hope this short list of what I consider to be must-haves will help you out.

Garden fork: Helpful for many gardening chores—from digging to planting to turning the soil to lifting tubers and dividing perennials—a fork is high on the list of necessary tools.

Hand pruner: My most frequently used gardening tool—there is almost always something that needs to be trimmed or pruned, and having a good pair of hand pruners is vitally important. I have four pairs of pruners, but I should probably eliminate two that have deteriorated because of poor-quality blades. My fallback is a pair of Felco bypass pruners that I've owned for at least a decade. Although they cost a little more money up front, you'll always appreciate how well they work and how they never appear to age. However, if you are the forgetful gardener and might misplace them—only to find them under a shrub the following spring—I suggest that you consider a less expensive option or purchase a pruner sheath (scabbard) or holster to keep them safe between snips.

Hoe: You're going to want to keep ahead of the thousands upon thousands of weed seeds that can sprout up—and using a hoe sure beats hand-picking.

Hose: I couldn't decide whether this was a basic or luxury item, as watering can always be done with a watering can…but I decided in favour of keeping it as a necessity, as it will save you a whole lot of time and effort.

Ladder: Whether or not it's considered a "garden tool," a ladder comes in very handy when dealing with taller trees and shrubs that need to be trimmed or sheared.

Long-handled, square-headed spades are best for heavy work, such as scooping loads of topsoil, because they are easier on your back. Short-handled, round-headed spades are better for digging smaller holes for planting.

Lopper: A pruner just won't cut it (literally and a good pun all in one) when it comes to removing big branches—and this is when you will be very glad you own a lopper.

Shears: Often plants don't need pruning; they need shearing. Although hand pruners are generally great for individual small-branch removal, shears are used to trim the exterior growth on hedges, small shrubs, annuals, perennials and groundcovers.

Shovel: What can I say? You know you're going to be planting something at some point or turning your garden, so a lightweight shovel is an integral part of the tool inventory. I highly recommend a fibreglass-handled version, because it's much lighter than one with a wood handle. Although the price tag is higher, it's worth it. The good news, though, is that just one shovel will do—you don't need a collection of six (like someone else I know…).

Springback rake: Usually about 18 in. (45 cm) wide with bendy tines, this simple tool makes tidying and raking waste from gardens and lawns quick and easy.

Luxury or secondary garden tools

If you don't have the space for a lot of tools or simply don't want to invest in "everything," here are some you can live without but are handy to have around. Or maybe you can just ask your neighbours to bulk up their tool inventory…

Compost turner: Actually, I suggest that this is a necessity if you have a compost box. A 3-ft. (90-cm) metal pole with a heavy-duty mechanical butterfly end that folds down when pushed into the compost and opens or expands

Opposite bottom: *Loppers are valuable for removing limbs that are thicker than your thumb. For heavy pruning jobs, choose the longer handled types for more torque.*

Use long-handled loppers to prune the lower branches of your fruit trees and pole pruners for the uppermost branches. Winter is the best time to tackle this job.

when pulled up, it mixes compost from below with the more recently added material. This helps to aerate the compost, which assists the decomposition process.

Extension bypass pruner: This pruner is mounted atop a pole with extension capabilities for those harder-to-reach branches.

Gloves: Although gloves aren't a necessity, they are very nice to have for quick and easy cleaning of your hands and fast removal when your cell phone rings. (Having said that, we're not supposed to have our cell with us in the garden, as gardening is meant to take us out of the hectic everyday for that small snippet of time. I have to admit, though, that I don't listen to my own advice on this one…) Anyway, I recommend a nitrile-coated gardening glove. Nitrile is a synthetic rubber that is very durable, waterproof and highly flexible, allowing you to work easily in the garden, even at the most delicate task, without the hindrance of a bulky glove.

Shrub rake: Similar to the springback rake but only about 10 in. (25 cm) wide, this variation is a good fit for use in and around flower beds. The 18-in. (45-cm) springback rake is often too wide to get around and under shrubs in the garden.

Spade: A flat-edged spade is great for edging garden beds or planting smaller annuals and perennials.

Sprinkler: Do you really need a sprinkler when you can hand-water? Well, the nice thing about sprinklers is that they water evenly. Smaller droplets for a longer period will do a better job of irrigating than hand-watering. Just make sure your child isn't near the tap while you situate your sprinkler. I thought I could trust my boy…

Waste bin: Although most of what we trim or need to dispose of from the garden should simply be put into the compost box, we do periodically need to put some material curbside for waste recycling. Grass clippings come to mind, as in the early spring we can have far too many for our compost boxes. A reusable plastic garbage can is a great means of transporting garden waste to the compost bin or, worst case, the curb.

Wheelbarrow: I seldom use my wheelbarrow, but I am very thankful that I have it to occasionally move heavy items around that would be a real problem to manage otherwise.

Vegetables

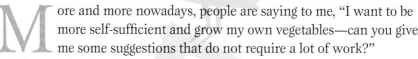

More and more nowadays, people are saying to me, "I want to be more self-sufficient and grow my own vegetables—can you give me some suggestions that do not require a lot of work?"

Thousands of gardeners are thinking about growing food…"I have a little space in my yard or deck, I *should* be growing some of my own produce and trying to live with sustainability in mind." But not all people realize that freezing and canning are vital to making the most of the edibles in your yard or community garden. Yup, back to the good old days when *I Love Lucy* reigned and pickle jars lined the pantry.

The biggest problem with our climate is that we can only grow healthy amounts of food crops for a period of six months and harvest for three to four. Okay, yes, we can grow some things year round—such as garlic and other root crops, and our Brussels sprouts may last until Christmas dinner—but I'm talking about the bulk of our harvesting. So the solution is storing, canning, pickling, drying and freezing. I believe it is imperative for those wanting to eat more from the garden to understand that the growing process is only part of the picture.

The good news is that you don't have to be a seasoned gardener to cut down on the number of trips to the produce aisle.

First, leaf vegetables such as chard and lettuce are no brainers. Peas, beans, zucchini—easy.

The list of crops that are easy to grow is long, so for the moment it's simpler to note the few that can be difficult to grow: eggplant, root crops and cole crops (excluding kale, which is super easy). Although these are not necessarily hard to grow, they're more prone to "issues."

Successful growing begins with good soil dug deeply in garden beds situated in a bright and sunny location. After that, regular watering and a balanced organic fertilizer mixed with the soil are the only other critical requirements.

ENSURING SUCCESS

How can I get the most crops from my vegetable garden?

Great question. I can give you one basic tip that should ensure you have success with your vegetable garden.

The old saying "You are what you eat" is a phrase that I like to reference whenever someone asks me for suggestions on how to improve their garden. So how does that statement relate to vegetable gardening?

Simply put, plant your crops in the best soil and mix of ingredients possible—and that, my friend, will guarantee you results.

Actually, I have one set of fingers crossed, because there is, admittedly, a little more to it. Plants do well when they can grow a deep root system into a rich blend of soil and other mediums and are supported by regular watering and addition of nutrients. So it's important to start off by mixing lots of good soil, manure and compost thoroughly with the existing soil.

When I say "mixing in," don't take it lightly. Often our yards are set on a base of construction fill or layer of hardpan, with only a small amount of soil placed over it in which to grow our lawns and gardens. Breaking through the fill or hardpan when adding the soil mix is vitally important for long-term success. Well, that is if you would like long, non-deformed carrots. If the carrot reaches down and encounters hardpan, it will grow sideways or become misshapen. All crops will be more successful when the root system can stretch downwards unobstructed. The deeper the better, because that's where the earth is cooler and water filters to, so that's where your vegetables can draw the necessary moisture for optimum growth.

Left: Encourage kids to grow it and they're more likely to eat it! No guarantees, though.

Right: A modestly sized backyard vegetable garden carved from existing lawn. It has enough square footage for a family to experiment, enjoy a nice mix of crops and have fun.

> To convert a patch of lawn 6 by 10 ft. (1.8 by 3 m) to a vegetable garden, I suggest thoroughly mixing in ½ yard (400 L) of soil and ¼ yard (200 L) each of manure and compost. Don't skimp. For the most part, this will be a one-time investment that you will enhance annually by adding approximately a quarter of the original mix.

The root of it all

Roots are like a car's radiator. Water passes through the radiator, circulates around the engine to cool it off, and then moves back to the radiator to be cooled off again.

A plant takes moisture from the earth, and this cools the leaves as it circulates through the entire plant and then back down to the roots. This process also replaces humidity that escapes the leaves through what is called transpiration.

So the deeper the roots can grow, the more cool moisture they'll be able to access, resulting in the healthiest and tastiest vegetables.

TOMATOES

I'd like to grow tomatoes—what varieties are most likely to be successful? What are your tricks for a great harvest?

Tomatoes are definitely the most popular of all vegetables grown in the garden…even though, technically, they are a fruit. You say "tomato," I say "tomahto"!

Tomatoes are easy to grow, but—as with any crop—they can have their challenges. To ensure you enjoy good results, it's most important to determine what varieties will do best in your garden. In every province, in every region and even in every yard, one variety will likely do better than another, as microclimates and soil composition can vary widely. Find out which ones do best in your own yard by testing a few different types over a number of years. I know many people who have done this and found a particular variety that works amazingly well in their garden and then stuck with it, saving seeds from the fruit each season.

I highly recommend you grow at least one cherry-tomato variety; 'Sweet 100' and 'Sweet Million' are my favourites. There's something about popping a bite-sized tomato, bursting with fresh-off-the-vine flavour, right into your mouth. Cherry tomatoes ripen early, quickly and continually, offering a ready-when-you-are crop for snacks and salads.

Larger slicing choices, such as the well-known 'Beefsteak', should really be limited to warmer summer areas, such as the interior of British Columbia and the Prairies. The big fruits require warm temperatures both day and night to vine ripen prior to the cool temperatures of fall.

West Coast gardens are best suited for medium-sized tomatoes, such as 'Fantastic', 'Early Girl', 'Oregon Spring', 'Better Boy' or a number of other common varieties proven suitable for a more temperate summer climate.

Don't try to grow any tomatoes, though, unless you have an extremely sunny spot in your yard or garden. Full sun all day would be best; however, a minimum of six hours of afternoon sun would support cherry- or medium-sized fruit. Resorting to fried green tomatoes in fall means failure in my opinion…but we'll blame Mother Nature for a cool summer if that does occur.

Tomatoes require a rich, deeply turned soil with plenty of mushroom manure (roughly 10 lb. or 4.5 kg per plant). Calcium is also an integral and essential element to prevent blossom end rot, a common issue in West Coast gardens. Mixing 1 cup (250 mL) of lime into the soil for each plant will usually prevent this deficiency.

PLANT IT RIGHT

Tomatoes can grow roots along their stem if planted deeply, enabling them to generate larger and stronger root systems that much more quickly. When planting a seedling, pinch off the bottom leaf or two, and then submerge the stem below the soil right to the leaf above the one(s) you just removed. The submerged stem will quickly root out, offering potential for the plant to grow faster and fruit more heavily.

LIMITED SPACE?

Reaching anywhere from 3–8 ft. (1–2.5 m), tomato plants take up a fair bit of garden real estate—and not just because of the elbow room they need for growing but also because of the way they can shade other vegetables.

This is where a few containers placed along the patio come in handy. With these, you can supply ample growing space for each plant and provide a great conversation piece right where you enjoy your summer dining. A container of at least 16 in. (40 cm) in diameter is required—and, as always, the bigger the better.

"Special" soil is not needed and, in fact, the same soil you use in the garden can fill your containers; mixed half and half with mushroom manure, it will provide a great blend for tomatoes. Although you can grow pretty much any tomato in a container, 'Patio' is particularly popular, with a stalky, firm posture and a height of about 3 ft. (90 cm), which make it relatively self-supporting as well as a very manageable size. Other varieties will likely need staking, and in a pot there isn't always enough depth to stabilize a lone pole holding up a massive tomato plant loaded with fruit. If support is needed, I suggest a tomato cage—the three or four pegs inserted into the soil make it a much more stable option.

Otherwise, tomatoes in containers require the same care as those grown in the ground.

Plump cherry tomatoes like these don't often make it to the table. They are picked and devoured on the spot!

You're probably thinking as you read this, "Hey Wim, are you this long-winded with all your answers?" Okay, I hear you…and yet there is still more to say about tomatoes. But they probably deserve it, since they are *the* most popular garden crop. Any extra tidbits of information can only assist you in getting even greater results. I promise you, though, that when I get to my answer regarding slugs, I'll be much briefer.

Maybe these wee tomatoes will make it into a Greek salad. You can't beat the taste of homegrown produce!

To support tomatoes growing in the garden, single staking is my preference, because you can sink a sturdy bamboo pole or cedar stake into the soil 2 ft. (60 cm) or more, providing ample support. When purchasing a stake for your tomato plants, remember that it must be 2–3 ft. (60–90 cm) longer than the height you expect your plant to grow in order to allow for that length needed below the soil.

Once planted and staked, the care and maintenance of a mature tomato plant needn't be onerous. Like any crop, regular water and nutrition is vital. Although you don't want to keep the soil continually moist, a thorough watering on sunny mornings is always a good idea. And I recommend doing a water test to see how fast your soil dries out. On a nice, sunny July morning, water your garden thoroughly. The next day, carefully scoop out a shovelful of soil. You want the soil to be moderately dry to at least a 4-in. (10-cm) depth. Do not water your garden again until it has sufficiently dried to that depth. It's important to let the roots of your crops search out moisture.

A DEEP TOPIC

The main purpose of roots is to search out moisture, which is the lifeline for any plant. Supply too much moisture and you are not making the roots work very hard—nor will they hunt! The larger and deeper the root system can grow, the better it is for the crop in every way. Taste, flavour, size, quality and texture are all affected by the plant's ability to support itself through stressful periods. Not stress like I have when I'm trying to meet a book deadline, but rather heat exhaustion, infestation, cold spells or drought. A robust root system helps the plant to endure these more effectively.

The pruning of "suckers" is an issue that elicits a strong response from many gardeners—some insist they remain, whereas others are adamant they must go. Defined as new growth between the main stem and a leaf or branch off that stem, a sucker is relatively easy to spot because of its upright growing habit.

Suckers ultimately sap energy from the mother plant, so even though they are capable of setting flowers and producing fruit, my view is that they should be removed to help the rest of the plant stay vibrant. I believe that too much strain can be placed on one root system and that the crop is better served by limiting how much it must support. On top of that, leaving the suckers on creates way too much greenery, shading the fruit on the plant. So remove those little suckers—simply pinch them off with your thumb and forefinger.

Finally, we haven't talked much about food. It can be called "nutrition" or "fertilizer," but I simply like to call it "food," as plants need to eat too. I recommend only organic fertilizer for anything we are growing for our consumption. And plants digest organic fertilizers more easily, so they get more benefit from the nutrition as well. There are a number of different fertilizers available in organic form, from liquid fish fertilizer to powdered bone meal, with granular blends specifically for vegetables being the least complicated method. They can be mixed with the soil when planting and then replenished on a monthly basis to provide any crop with all the food it needs.

So the last thing you need to think about now is…just how *are* you going to use all those bushels of tomatoes that you'll be harvesting?

CHOOSING SEEDS OR PLANTS

I want to grow a vegetable garden—should I start my veggies from seed or buy starter plants?

Q.

A. There are two reasons for a gardener to grow vegetables from seed. Starting from seed is much more economical than going with pre-grown plants. Naturally, though, there is additional work involved and some space required inside your home.

The second big motivator is variety, with a much larger assortment of vegetables available from seed than in plant form.

Chances are that even if you buy some starts from your local garden centre, you will still want to grow some from seed, as not everything is available as plants.

Timing can vary drastically on when to start sowing each vegetable, either indoors or out. Check the seed package for information about when and how best to sow. Many seeds are extremely small, even tinier than a pinhead, so look deeply into some of those little envelopes…they *are* in there!

Vegetables I highly recommend you sow from seed indoors:

- Beets*
- Bok Choy
- Broccoli*
- Brussels sprouts*
- Cabbage*
- Cauliflower*
- Kale*
- Leeks*
- Lettuce
- Parsnip*
- Peas*
- Spinach*
- Turnips*

Starting these vegetables indoors early will allow you to jump-start the season, as they are cool-weather crops and can be planted out early.

Vegetables to sow from seed directly outdoors:

- Arugula
- Asparagus
- Beans
- Bok Choy**
- Brussels sprouts**
- Carrots
- Celery
- Corn
- Garlic
- Kale**
- Lettuce**
- Onions
- Peas**
- Potatoes
- Radish
- Shallots
- Spinach**

**Although these vegetables are also listed in the sow-indoors section, you can direct-sow outdoors mid and late season for additional late-summer and fall crops.*

Vegetables to consider buying in plant form, as you may want more than one variety or only one or two plants for the garden:

- Cucumber
- Eggplant
- Pepper
- Pumpkin
- Tomato
- Watermelon
- Winter Squash
- Zucchini

Top: *Lettuce starters like these are best for growing in mixed vegetable planters with an assortment of other vegetables. They could also be grown individually in pots.*

Middle: *Red onions can be started from seed, sets or starters. They look great in a salad and also store quite well.*

Bottom: *These little pumpkin starters are a perfect size for a small city garden. Pumpkins take up a lot of real estate, so plant only one to three plants at the most; otherwise, it could get spooky.*

HARVESTING

I've had success with my vegetable garden this year—when should I be harvesting?

Q.

A. The how and when of harvesting is, of course, dependent on the crop, but here are some basic guidelines.

Some crops are obvious, like tomatoes, for example. Harvest tomatoes as they start to ripen and turn red, and if necessary you can even pick them when they are still a bit green and let them mature inside the house. If you don't keep an eye on them, there is a risk you will be leaving your tomato on the vine for too long and will lose it. This may sound obvious, but sometimes planning is required to maximize the benefit of your homegrown crop and prevent simply having to give most of it away to the neighbours. They will come to expect buckets of tomatoes and barrels of zucchini, so you might want to be cautious about how generous you are…Do you have a big batch of tomatoes starting to ripen? Then you might want to plan on making a few batches of canned tomatoes or simply eating a lot of salads.

Even planning for a crop like lettuce can be necessary. They look so cute and puppy-like the week after planting, but four to six weeks down the road you've got yourself a dozen St. Bernards in your garden.

Root crops can be the easiest to manage. In more temperate parts of the country, where cold temperatures don't arrive until well into November or December, you can simply leave them in the ground, where they'll remain cool and moist, keeping them healthy right through winter. Just harvest them as needed, gently lifting them out with a spading fork. The main concern is that the crops shouldn't freeze. You can add protection by covering the soil around your crops with a 6-in. (15-cm) layer of straw to minimize the cold penetrating the soil. Once harvesting is complete, you can mix the mulch right into the soil to improve it for next year's garden.

Enjoy your harvest through the winter by canning, drying or freezing. It feels great to still be eating your homegrown crops long after summer has ended, even if it is only some dried herbs.

Cold comfort

The great benefit of leaving root and cole crops—or any crop for that matter—in the ground for as long as possible is that the chilly weather forces each veggie to build up antifreeze within itself as protection from the cold. This antifreeze is basically sugar—so some of the tastiest crops in the garden result when vegetables have endured chilly temperatures.

WINTER VEGETABLES

Q.

What vegetables can I plant as winter crops?

Above: Broccoli should be harvested when the heads are large but before they go to seed (indicated by small yellow flowers emerging from the head). Cut the centre broccoli head off, but leave the stalk, as new smaller flowerets will grow from it.

A. Depending on how cold it gets where you live, there are a number of crops you can consider growing for a winter harvest.

In mild areas, temperatures that remain in the 32–50F (0–10C) range allow the gardener to grow a host of different crops throughout the fall and winter months, even if the temperatures periodically dip to a non-prolonged -14F (-10C).

There are some crops that you can simply leave in the soil from your spring planting and then harvest as you need them over the winter. The most common are carrots, beets, parsnips, garlic, rutabagas, globe onions and even potatoes (though they are a little more tender). If you're concerned about frost penetrating the ground for extended periods, insulate your crops by mulching the garden with straw, leaves or any other light material that can simply be dug into the soil later. Or simply harvest your crops when a cold spell hits and store them in a cool place.

Right: Who says vegetable beds have to be square?

There are also crops above ground that can soldier on come the colder weather of fall and winter. Kale, Brussels sprouts, cabbage, cauliflower, leeks, some larger bean varieties and Swiss chard are among the above-ground crops that can remain in the garden through fall and winter. If you decide in the summer that you would like more in your garden for the upcoming cold season, go ahead and sow extra of any of these veggies—just do it by mid August and have the seedlings ready for planting by the beginning of September. You want the plants to be relatively mature come the first frost.

Lastly, there are some crops that don't mind cool temperatures, though they won't last through the winter. Still, they are a nice addition to the fall garden if you have space. We'll call these ones marginally hardy crops, with some of the most common being cabbage, leaf lettuce, collards, mustard, spinach and radish.

Remember that some of the best flavour comes from our winter garden crops, which boost up their sugar content as protection from the cold—so don't miss the opportunity to enjoy some of the tastiest veggies of the year (see page 42).

And please don't waste the leaves or stalks as you harvest. When you pick your Brussels sprouts or broccoli or carrots and have all those leaves and stems left over, remember they are rich in vitamins and minerals and add them to a smoothie, add a few to soup stock or rinse and freeze them for future use.

Top: For success with garlic, plant in early fall so that they can root on during the winter and be well established come spring.

Bottom: A small bed of assorted varieties of kale is perfect for the gardener and cook. Simply pull off enough leaves for each meal, and they will always replenish themselves.

YAY, KALE!

Kale is one of the most prized vegetables in my garden, as it is super nutritious with large amounts of vitamins, minerals and fibre. I also love the fact that it is so versatile in the kitchen—great for soups, stews, stir-fries and more—and that it can be available fresh from the garden pretty much 12 months a year. You never really have to harvest the plant, except for removal from the garden the following spring to make room for new plants. I simply pinch off however many leaves I need for my cooking requirements.

ROOFTOP GARDENING

Q. *I would like to have a fruit and vegetable container garden on my rooftop patio—what do you suggest I grow?*

A. Although root veggies and cole crops (with the exception of super-easy kale) do not grow well in containers, most leaf vegetables, tomatoes, peppers, eggplants, beans and peas, along with many herbs and berries and even some dwarf fruit trees, do just fine. But leave the corn to the fields of Chilliwack.

When you're considering the vessels (containers or planters), think big. The bigger the better, to ensure success. A larger container will help prevent the soil from going dry, which could greatly hinder growth or even kill the plants. Light-coloured containers work best, as dark-coloured pots absorb the sun and heat the soil, which is detrimental to many vegetables.

Fill the planters with a mix of good-quality soil and manure, along with coco fibre/coir (my preference) or peat moss. Mix in a healthy amount of granular organic fertilizer, tuck in the vegetable or fruiting plant, and then… just add water. Regular watering is vital. Ensure your containers have sufficient drain holes for excess moisture to escape through. Usually a minimum of three drain holes is required for any pot over 16 in. (40 cm) wide.

***Left**: Peppers are perfectly suited to container growing, as they are not overly large plants and, as a rule, do not require supports. Place them in a hot, sunny location.*

***Right**: This planter has a combination of herbs (basil), fruit (strawberries) and vegetables (lettuce). They coexist well and provide cooks with a little bit of everything.*

Although saucers catch the overflow that drains out of a pot or container, elevating containers just slightly off the ground with pot feet or risers will ensure water drains out and away. This is important because plants can suffer when the roots are surrounded by excess water—it can even rot their roots.

Maximize your container space by planting smaller-growing vegetables like lettuce, fruiting plants such as strawberries, or low-growing or creeping herbs like oregano in and around a taller-growing vegetable such as a tomato. Herbs, vegetables and edible flowers can all grow together, making a very attractive container display.

FLOWER FLAVOUR

When planting food crops in large containers, add additional interest by tucking in some edible flowers. This will also help to attract pollinators, in addition to making your garden more beautiful.

Edible flowers are just that—flowers that you can eat without worry or harm. Just because you can eat them, however, doesn't mean that they all taste as good as they look. Nevertheless, they do make a wonderful garnish or liven up the presentation of any culinary dish. Use them in salads, jellies, drinks, honey and more.

Edible flowers can also be preserved for future consumption—dry or freeze them, or steep them in oil, which also looks stunning. My favourite way to preserve edible flowers is to dip them in a thoroughly blended mixture of 1 Tbsp. (15 mL) sugar to one egg white (to sidestep any concerns about ingesting raw egg, you can use powdered egg white mixed with water according to package directions). Allow the flowers to dry completely and crystallize for a wonderful treat or garnish.

Here are my top edible-flower picks:

- Artichoke
- Borage
- Calendula
- Chamomile
- Chive
- Chrysanthemum
- Citrus
- Clover
- Dandelion
- Daylily
- Elderflower
- Hibiscus
- Jasmine
- Lilac
- Nasturtium (flower and seed)
- Pansy
- Rose (flower and hip)
- Sunflower (flower and seeds)
- Violet
- Zucchini (flower and fruit)

Top to bottom: *sunflower, borage flower and nasturtium.*

LETTUCE

Q. *How do I avoid bitter, bolting lettuce?*

A. A lettuce that is going straight to flowering has been very stressed and is telling you it needs more room; good nutrition such as fish fertilizer, compost tea or a granular organic; and regular watering (every second to third day, depending on how hot the weather is). All lettuces prefer cool conditions and lots of growing space. Big butter lettuces need a good foot between them. I love the beautiful 'Esmeralda' butterhead lettuce—never bitter and always tender and delicious.

Butter lettuce makes wonderful salads and can also be found in sandwiches in my kitchen!

Although some varieties of lettuce, and more particularly butter lettuce, can tolerate heat and even greenhouse conditions, most prefer a sunny, open-air garden setting.

There is no doubt that we all have our lettuce preference, but why not expand your love for lettuce by growing one of the so many different varieties of butter, leaf, head and romaine? Use the large iceberg leaves for a wrap-style meal, romaine for a great Caesar salad that includes the delicious heart, and the velvet-soft leaves of the butter lettuce for something a little more elegant.

LETTUCES TO LOVE

- **'Romaine Cylindrical':** upright heads; the long, cupped, medium-green leaves are thick and very crisp with a mild flavour that is even on the sweet side (65–85 days to maturity).

- **'Buttercrunch':** Heavy, compact heads; superb flavour and heat resistant (60–70 days to maturity).

- **Mesclun Mix:** Mesclun is the French name for mixed young salad leaves (50–70 days to maturity).

- **'Prize Head':** This leafy lettuce has large upright, light-green crumpled leaves with pretty bronze edges (45–55 days to maturity).

- **Iceberg:** A medium-sized head with fringed green leaves that give way to tender blanching, almost-white hearts (75 days to maturity).

CUCUMBERS

My cucumbers are always bitter—what causes this?

Q.

A. I've heard this lament before. Out in your garden, you scout out that perfect cucumber for tonight's dinner, but there really isn't a lot of scouting to do because we always know exactly where the big one is. Snip. Off comes that long, slender, dark-green cuke. Mmmmmm. The work is done and now it's time to enjoy! The family marvels as you haul the specimen into the kitchen. You're a leave-the-skin-on kind of cuke eater—particularly when it is from your own organic garden—and so, after a quick rinse, it's time for the ceremonial first slice.

Well, okay, the first slice was the butt end and it was a bit bitter, but now it's time for the good part. You raise the thick slice to your mouth in anticipation of that magical bite.

Although they're not quite sure what it was that you exclaimed, the whole family knows it wasn't pleasant.

All that hard work—planting, weeding, feeding and watering—for this end result…*a bitter cucumber*. It's almost like a bad movie. You know the one that ends and you're sitting there numbly thinking, "What, that's it!?"

Choose cucumber types from among varieties such as pickling, bush, telegraph, burpless and sandwich. They are an easy crop even for novice gardeners!

Cucumbers contain a compound called cucurbitacin (say that fast 10 times). Scientists have not yet determined exactly why it becomes so pronounced, but they have discovered that cucurbitacin is more prevalent in fruit and foliage if the plant has been stressed from heat and drought. The hotter it is—and the more the plant dries—the greater the content of cucurbitacin. Even a partial drying for a short period can affect the cucurbitacin content. And the more cucurbitacin, the more bitter the cuke.

So, what to do? The time to prevent bitterness in your cucumbers is well before harvest.

Everyone has to grow a zucchini plant once in their life, just for the experience. Nothing produces the sheer poundage of food like the wonderful zucchini. Be brave enough to try one, and then start looking for recipes!

The leaves are growing large and the fruit are developing, which means the plant is going to require plentiful watering to maintain a healthy level of moisture. In cooler weather 2–3 in. (5–7.5 cm) at least twice a week suffices, but I recommend daily irrigation in warm temperatures, as long as the water drains through the soil. That's not the whole picture, though. Mulching as the plants mature is also crucial. Building a 4-in. (10-cm) deep layer of mulch radiating 3 or 4 ft. (90 or 120 cm) from the main stem of the plant will greatly assist in preventing the soil from drying. The cucumber will also shoot a few additional roots up into the mulch, enabling it to more readily absorb water. Mulch can be composed of additional soil, compost, coco fibre or straw, or any combination of these materials.

And one last tip: acidic soil has also been found to increase the content of cucurbitacin. Adding organic lime to your cucumber patch at a ratio of 10 lb. (4.5 kg) per 200 sq. ft. (18.5 sq. m) annually prior to planting will also help to prevent a bitter harvest.

Oh, and if you're thinking of pickling those bitter cukes, don't bother. The end result will simply be bitter pickled cucumbers.

ZUCCHINIS

Q. *My zucchinis start to rot just after they have formed—what am I doing wrong?*

A. How are you going to make all that zucchini bread, zucchini loaf, zucchini cake, zucchini stew, zucchini soup, baked zucchini, fried zucchini, grilled zucchini and deep-fried zucchini without the never-ending crop that can come from even just one zucchini plant? And don't forget the disappointed neighbourhood!

One thing I tell people when they say they want to plant zucchini is that they may just need one plant. The exception is if you're like me and enjoy baby zucchini grilled on the barbecue. Then, more plants are in order, as you'll be harvesting them very frequently, at 6 in. (15 cm) or even smaller.

The rotting zucchini is not because of something you're doing—it might, however, be the result of something you're not doing. Zucchinis require high levels of calcium; otherwise, they commonly fall victim to a disease called blossom end rot. I think that everyone who has grown zucchini has experienced this, along with the other disease, zucchini-*abundantitus*. That's when zucchini is rotting in the garden simply because you cannot bear to eat any more zucchini!

The solution to blossom end rot is simple. You must get more calcium into that plant. The only problem is that it takes some time for calcium to become available within the soil so that it is accessible to what is growing in it.

One of the best sources of calcium is organic lime. Lime does something else, though. As it adds the necessary elements calcium (Ca) and magnesium (Mg) to the soil, it also raises the pH level. Raising the pH of the soil increases its alkalinity. This can be good in areas with chronically low pH levels and not so good where pH tends to be a little above neutral.

You may want to complete a soil test prior to adding the lime. If your soil pH is 6.5 or lower, then using lime is a quick and easy way to increase the calcium content. Add roughly 10 lb. (4.5 kg) per 200 sq. ft. (18.5 sq. m) in both October and March.

The zucchini bloom is sought after by chefs, to be battered, deep fried and then exorbitantly priced.

If your soil tests at 7 or higher, then you may want to save those eggshells that you would normally send to the compost box. Adding baked and crushed eggshells is a quick way to increase the calcium in your soil without dramatically changing the pH level. Simply bake a cookie sheet of eggshells at 350F for approximately 20–30 minutes, and then let them cool. Anytime after that, you can crush them with a rolling pin. Scatter and scratch 1 cup (250 mL) of the crushed shells evenly into the soil around each zucchini in a circumference of 1–3 ft. (30–90 cm). This should definitely cure your zucchini of blossom end rot.

GOLDEN TOUCH

Traditional green zucchini is by far the most popular, but for variety and a touch of colour, the golden, speckled, or globe types are just as easy to grow. Most of these are only available from seed.

Fruits & Berries

As fashion changes through the years, so do people's needs and wants in the garden. My bell-bottomed pants and high-heeled boots may come back into fashion, but it might be a wiser choice for me to just retire them. Fruiting trees, vines and bushes, however, just continue to become more and more hip. Increasingly, gardeners want a little slice of the farm in their own backyard or on their patio or even among their flower beds.

And it's not only classics such as raspberries, strawberries and blueberries that are in demand. More and more people are looking for goji and aronia berries, olive and pomegranate trees, honeyberries and any other health-benefitting crop that has surfaced as a miracle food guaranteed to extend your life or cure what ails you.

Having said that, anyone who has a bit of garden space or room for pots on their patio has a wonderful opportunity to harvest even a small amount of fresh produce right in their own backyard. And what could be more healthy (or delicious) than that? Don't forget that fruits and berries are among the most profuse crops that can be grown—what better way to assist our fragile environment than by producing as much as we can in our own gardens, rather than buying what is hauled in from far-off lands by diesel-guzzling mega-trucks or cargo ships?

When you're considering fruits and berries, think long term. Once they're planted in your yard, many fruit trees and berry bushes can produce abundant crops for 50 years or more, with very little effort required from you.

As yard sizes continue to shrink, the demand for multi-graft fruit trees has been rising. Few of us have room for an orchard, but it's probably possible to squeeze in a couple of dwarf or semi-dwarf fruit trees. And what better way to enjoy the sense of an orchard harvest than with a plum, cherry or apple tree that has four varieties ripening consecutively through the season?

From my row of raspberries to my Asian apple pear to my multi-graft plum tree, it is the fruits and berries that make up the most rewarding part of my garden.

Opposite: High in fibre and antioxidants, the raspberry has remained a favourite of Canadian gardeners for years. Many varieties are available, including a golden raspberry.

CHOOSING FRUITS AND BERRIES

What is the easiest fruit tree to grow for guaranteed results?

Fruit trees in general are not all that hard to grow, and you don't necessarily need a great big yard to have one, two or more fruit trees. At my home, on my lot of 60 by 150 ft. (18 by 46 m), I have an Asian apple pear, a 'Cox Orange' apple, a three-in-one plum and two 'Colonnade' (columnar) apple trees. And I could fit even a couple more fruit trees into my yard if I wished.

Often when we think of a fruit tree, we envision a massive giant taking up the majority of a small backyard. The fruit trees produced for market in this day and age, however, are not those colossal varieties best suited for pastures or acreage.

Growers produce trees nowadays that are classified as semi-dwarf and reach a maximum height of about 15 ft. (4.5 m)—a lot shorter than their relatives of yesteryear that reached 50 ft. (15 m). These semi-dwarf trees are produced by grafting a not-so-vigorous understock or rootstock to the whip (the above-ground part) of the fruit-tree variety.

Without a doubt, the easiest fruit tree to grow depends on where you reside. With the diverse climate and microclimates across the country, some species do better than others in different regions. In the Southern Okanagan of BC, peach trees are a relatively low-maintenance and great-producing crop, making a juicy harvest easy to achieve. Try growing a peach tree in Metro Vancouver and you'll be lucky to pick a handful of small and not-so-juicy fruit. This is mostly due to the region's cooler temperatures and excessive rainfall.

If you're looking for simple, then I recommend you grow an apple tree no matter where you live, as throughout North America they are easy to grow with almost guaranteed results.

If space is an issue, try growing a dwarf fruit tree in a pot.
Jay Shaw photo

But even that advice comes with a caveat. Success with each type of apple tree varies somewhat from region to region. The 'McIntosh', for example, does much better in a warmer summer climate than a more moderate zone—for which I would recommend a 'Gala' or 'Honeycrisp'. So choose the variety for your area carefully by checking with your local garden centre.

My second recommendation is a plum tree, which is also easy to grow and usually supplies an abundance of fruit. The limitation of the plum is that the fruit doesn't have the longevity of the apple, and so for a nice easy-to-grow and long-lasting crop, the decision is simple.

Plus, an apple a day keeps the doctor away! (I just made that up—and you're welcome to use it.)

Q. *I am trying to integrate berry fruits into my garden—what's easy and attractive?*

A. First of all, don't plant anything you don't enjoy eating. I could recommend many different fruiting bushes—such as loganberry, for example—but I don't want to hear you say, "I don't like loganberries." Actually, the truth is that you could pretty much plant any fruiting bush or crop in your landscape garden as long as it gets enough sun and aesthetically fits in.

I think I can offer one suggestion that will most definitely satisfy your wishes.

I have never heard anyone say they don't enjoy blueberries. By the way, I'd like to know who the literary master was that came up with the name… uhhh, it's blue and a berry…so let's call it…

But name aside, blueberries are a perfect addition to virtually any landscape or container garden for many different reasons. First on the list is that you're going to get one of the most nutritious and tasty crops possible—and for an extended period. Once they start fruiting in summer, blueberries continue to do so for at least a month and up to two, depending on variety.

Before you start planting, though, it's important to know that it takes two to tango. In other words, there needs to be two different varieties within relatively close proximity to cross-pollinate. If your neighbour has a blueberry bush, that will likely suffice to pollinate what you have on your side of the fence. And it's not like borrowing their ladder, so you don't have to return anything. As a general rule, the closer your blueberry bush is to another blueberry bush, the better the pollination and the more productive your plants will be.

If you plant two, though, it would be wise to select both an early-ripening and a late-ripening variety to achieve a long fruiting period through summer. Choose well and you will be able to pick a bowlful of berries every morning for breakfast from July right through September.

Blueberries can be region specific, so consult your local garden centre about suitable varieties for your region.

And don't just plant blueberries anywhere in your garden. They do best in a very sunny spot, but ensure that you strategically plant them in a location where you won't need to walk over other plants to get at the fruit.

I have three blueberry plants and enjoy great success with this easy-to-grow shrub. Once blueberries start producing—usually the first year after planting—you can enjoy crops for up to 50 years from that same plant. And based on their health benefits, eating fresh-from-your-garden blueberries might just ensure that you'll be around for the life of your plant.

You can fit a blueberry bush just about anywhere, like this one planted in front of my gazebo.

BERRIED TREASURE

Blueberry plants make an incredible addition to any landscape because of their ongoing attributes:

Spring: Lush, bright-green foliage and clusters of white bell-shaped flowers.

Summer: Clusters of attractive and delicious berries.

Fall through winter: Toward the year's end, the branches of this deciduous shrub turn a bronzy red. You can take advantage of this and prune your blueberries (see page 201) to use the cuttings in festive floral displays indoors or in any of the soil-filled containers on your patio that need a pick-me-up.

Quite possibly the easiest fruit to grow, blueberries are a must-have in your garden! They require little attention, little space, and they reward amply. Don't forget, you'll need two different varieties for pollination.

BIGGER BERRIES

I get decent berry crops but the fruit is not as big, juicy and sweet as I had hoped—is there something that I should be feeding them?

Q.

A. I often say that plants are what they're growing in and to have success with pretty much any plant, you must ensure there is an appropriate amount of soil to accommodate a healthy root system.

Obviously, a strawberry plant doesn't need a large planting hole, but a blueberry bush that can grow to a height of 6 ft. (1.8 m) definitely does. The deeper and wider a planting hole you can provide—filled with a wide assortment of soil amendments—the better the all-round performance of your berry crop will be.

Water is the next most important contributor to plump and juicy fruit. Once a berry has formed and is starting to develop, it is imperative the plant be supported with regular watering. Just one period of drying out as the fruit is on its way to maturity will damage the plant.

Help prevent the crop from drying out by adding mulch once every year in spring. I recommend that you add a layer at least 1 in. (2.5 cm) thick for small plants such as strawberries and up to 6 in. (15 cm) for larger blueberry or raspberry bushes. Apply this layer evenly right out to the plant's drip line. The mulch will help to retain moisture by offering additional depth of medium, whether it be soil, compost, manure or something else, insulating the plant's roots from the warm, dry summer air. Most berry crops will also shoot up roots into mulch, expanding the plant's ability to absorb moisture and nutrients, improving its health and correspondingly increasing the quantity and size of the fruit.

Lastly, fertilizer will help to improve plant structure, pest resistance and yields. Granular organic fertilizer applied in early spring, with supplemental in-season liquid feeding of fish fertilizer and/or liquid seaweed on a monthly basis from May through September, will also improve the welfare of the plant. it's not the fertilizer itself that will improve your berry size or yield; it's that

Blackberries have a long history in North America. They were used for medicinal purposes and as a healthy food source by indigenous peoples and early settlers. And really, who doesn't like blackberry pie?

the fertilizer will ensure a healthy plant. And healthy plant equals healthy crop.

The healthy plant that results from readily available nutrition, regular watering and a bright sunny spot with plenty of soil in which to grow a large root system will have no trouble producing those bountiful crops you are hoping for.

The root of it all

When planting fruiting trees or bushes, ensure that you invest in a wide assortment of soil amendments. I recommend mixing the following with the existing soil:

22 lb. (10 kg) manure

2 cu. ft. (56 L) coir or peat moss

22 lb. (10 kg) compost and/or soil

22 lb. (10 kg) fine mulch (to aerate the existing soil and make it easy for the tree to grow a root system quickly into the fresh material as opposed to having to break through clay-based conditions or any form of hardpan)

Mix the above ingredients with the existing soil thoroughly to a depth of 3 ft. (90 cm) by a width of 3 ft. (90 cm).

CONTAINER GARDENING

Q.

I would like to grow strawberries in a container and want ever-bearing plants with the largest berry possible—what should I choose?

Above: Here I'm adding compost around the base of my raspberry canes to add nutrition and improve soil moisture retention. Jay Shaw photo

A. Strawberries do very well in containers, so your success should be guaranteed. Well, this is not a personal guarantee…but I do believe you will enjoy great results.

The category of ever-bearing strawberries includes only a few varieties—none have excessively large fruit but all are sweet. I recommend you plant a medium-sized cultivar called 'Tri-Star' from the day-neutral category.

Day-neutral varieties are similar in almost every way to regular ever-bearing varieties with one big exception. Traditional ever-bearing choices only fruit the first four weeks or so of July, whereas the day-neutral varieties can produce from May through to the frost. The end result is that you can enjoy much more fruit than the traditional ever-bearing varieties.

The term "day-neutral" refers to this category of strawberry's ability to flower continuously because of their insensitivity to daylight length, which is the factor that controls flower production in other strawberries.

Day-neutral strawberries are relatively hardy and will normally survive through winters in a temperate climate. In colder regions, they should be mulched with 6 in. (15 cm) of straw or leaves for protection if they're in the garden. If they're grown in containers, it would be wise to find a sheltered spot to overwinter them, or simply place them in an enclosed cool garage. Check monthly to ensure the soil is not going too dry.

Strawberries require as much sun as possible, along with good air circulation. I also recommend you grow them at the edge of the container so that the fruit and runners (baby plants, so to speak) can spill over the side. You can trim the runners off to offer more energy and production capability to the mother plant or simply enjoy the look of the runners spilling over the side of your container. Come fall, you can snip them off the mother plant to increase your strawberry population or to pot up and offer to friends and family. Who wouldn't want a strawberry plant?

Provide your plants with a rich mix of soil, manure and coir or peat moss and ensure they are watered regularly in season.

Left: There are two types of strawberries: ever bearing and June bearing. Grow a few of each type to have a continuous supply of fruit.
Right: Strawberries grow well in hanging baskets, making them a good choice for an apartment dweller with a small balcony. Adequate sun and moisture are the most important requirements.

Q.

I love fresh raspberries but only have a patio—can they be grown in containers? And are there any berries particularly good for growing in pots?

A. Berry crops in containers are definitely more of a challenge to grow than those in the ground. Much of this has to do with the roots being restricted by the pot size, along with the stress that can be placed on the plant by the roots heating up within the container during warm periods.

Many fruits and berries are simply not suitable for containers, based on their growth habits. In general, raspberries in a container would grow too tall and have a tendency to flop over. Raspberries are one of those berry crops best kept in the traditional long rows of a garden setting. it's the old saying "Right plant, right place." Or "Don't try to fit a square peg into a round hole." But what if the square peg is small and the round hole very large? In other words, are there exceptions to this rule?

Actually, in this case, the answer is yes—there are certain raspberry varieties that work well in pots. I don't often get specific with cultivars; however, there is one worth a special mention.

A new variety called 'Raspberry Shortcake' is shorter growing and thornless and developed to provide a good harvest of large, juicy and sweet fruit right from a pot on your balcony. The plant reaches a maximum height of 2–3 ft. (60–90 cm) and in just two growing seasons can fill a 20-in. (50-cm) pot with canes that should continue to produce for years.

To add to your container crop experience, you may also want to consider

Above: *March is the season for planting berries. Although raspberries are not usually grown in pots, the 'Raspberry Shortcake' variety thrives in them.*
Rob Paasch, Fisher Farms LLC photo

Right: *This thornless, self-fertile raspberry yields plump and delicious fruit mid summer. Grow it in a large pot with strawberries underplanted for a double delight!*
Rob Paasch, Fisher Farms LLC photo

a blueberry. One that is great in containers is 'Sunshine'. Growing to about 3 ft. (90 cm), it makes a nice, manageable plant suited to patios.

I recommend taking advantage of the space at the base of either of these crops by planting some strawberry companions. Most strawberries work well at the edge of a container, allowing you to get maximum benefit from your growing space. An ever-bearing day-neutral variety (see page 56) can offer fruit throughout the entire summer. One 'Raspberry Shortcake' or 'Sunshine' blueberry, along with four to six ever-bearing or day-neutral strawberry plants, will provide you with fresh fruit additions to any salad, spring through summer. That's if they make it to the kitchen.

KEEP IN MIND…

> Slightly more care is required when growing in containers. Crops need constant moisture and don't tolerate drying periods well. Regular nutrition from organic liquid fertilizer and a monthly compost-tea treatment will not only give you great crops but also a healthy and attractive patio plant.

Imagine a pot with an apple tree just outside your back door. You'll quickly be hooked on container fruit gardening when you see bounty like this!

I would like an apple tree suitable for a container—any suggestions?

Q.

A. Fruit trees in containers are not something I normally recommend, with the exception of some true dwarf varieties or the 'Colonnade' apple trees.

'Colonnade' apples are columnar trees that grow to about 12 ft. (3.6 m) but can be kept to 6 ft. (1.8 m). You should have success growing them in containers—that is, big containers that are a minimum of 24 in. (60 cm) wide and as deep. Usually the harvests are small, so it's more of a novelty plant with a possible crop size of 10 1b. (4.5 kg) per tree per year.

Fruit trees are best placed in a location that is sunny in the afternoon as opposed to the early morning, when the sun is weaker.

NEW TREES

 My new small apple tree just planted this spring is covered in fruit. Should I let it all mature or pull some off so that the tree's energy goes into its root development instead?

A. Your apple tree will most likely self-thin within the month. If not, I suggest you pick off some of the apples in early July. The purpose is to lessen the weight on a small tree as opposed to a concern about reducing its energy. Allowing just two or three pieces of fruit per cluster would reduce the strain on branches that could bend easily under the weight. This advice holds true mostly for apples and pears because of their size and weight.

A healthy amount of fruit is left on this tree.

Thinning (or culling, as it's sometimes called) ensures the growth of larger fruit and lessens the weight borne by branches. In Holland, they will cull up to 50 percent of the fruit of various crops.

PRUNING PROBLEM

I have a large and healthy cherry tree that was pruned last year. It has a fine crop of leaves but only a few cherries—what should I do to get more? My neighbour has a neglected cherry tree that produces a huge fruit crop!

Q.

A. With almost any fruit tree, there is a certain amount of maintenance required, including pruning, feeding, pest control and periodic evaluation. But it sounds like you've got that under control.

The reason you don't have much fruit this year may be a result of excessive pruning. An aggressive pruning is an important step in maintaining a fruit tree; however, it should be done only on a periodic basis to rejuvenate the tree. I suggest once every four or five years.

Another cause of a poor cherry crop is premature fruit drop. This is where the fruit forms but drops off the tree when the cherries are very small. This can be a result of poor pollination or a lack of minerals and micronutrients, more specifically iron.

I don't think your issue would be poor pollination, because you have another prolific cherry tree close by.

To rectify a possible iron deficiency, I recommend adding fritted trace elements every year or two. At the drip line of the tree (the outer leaves are classified as the drip line area), insert a crowbar or similar device to make a hole 2–3 in. (5–7.5 cm) deep in which to drop 1 Tbsp. (15 mL) of the fritted trace elements. Repeat this every 2–3 ft. (60–90 cm) around the drip line.

If you only have room to grow one cherry tree, make it a lapin cherry. They are self-fertile, resistant to cracking and, of course, delicious.

Herbs

I n the past, when cooking up a meal, I might have checked out the spice drawer and pulled out a dried seasoning or two to sprinkle into the stew bubbling on the stove or casserole going into the oven. And I never added a spice or herb to salads. How things change.

Now, home cooks are accustomed to incorporating fresh herbs and spices into everyday recipes. it's not only that we're buying more fresh herbs from our local grocery store, but we're also growing more in our gardens and on our patios—and for good reason. There's nothing fresher tasting than seasonings just picked from outside your back door.

I've watched herb sections at garden centres grow from just a couple of plants, such as parsley and chives, to a collection more than 100 varieties strong. Nowadays, you will see multiple varieties of oregano, tarragon, cilantro, thyme, stevia, sage and so much more. And don't forget the queen of all herbs—basil—in an assortment of different varieties, from green to globe to purple to spicy.

The astounding growth in herb popularity has been propelled by the younger generation's booming awareness of the connections between cooking and gardening and their huge interest in creating unforgettable "foodie" experiences for friends and family in an inexpensive, sustainable way. I am inspired by the enthusiasm of younger couples as they circle the gigantic herb benches in my garden centres, and their anticipation of lush herb planters is a reminder of how much a small garden can heighten the pleasures of simple day-to-day living.

Opposite: Start harvesting basil more frequently when it begins flowering to encourage additional growth and crop.

Growing herbs is only part of the process. Drying and preserving are as important so that we can enjoy the flavours and aromas throughout the year.

HELPING HERBS SURVIVE WINTER

Q. *I love Mediterranean herbs such as rosemary and lavender but sometimes lose them in the winter—how can I ensure their survival?*

A. Many herbs are perennial in parts of the country where the temperatures are not too nippy through the winter. And others can also be protected from cold spells if they are kept in pots and brought into a chilled but frost-free area or heavily mulched out in the garden or even draped with burlap (see page 66).

Bay leaf, curry, lavender, mint, rosemary, sage, savory and tarragon are the most popular examples of herbs that are perennial and capable of surviving non-extreme North American winters. Often people will grow these herbs in containers so that they can provide shelter November through March by moving them closer to the house or into a greenhouse—or, for periods of extreme cold, by placing plants for a month or so in an enclosed cool garage, even if there are no windows. It's important to check the soil of any plant

Lavender thrives in hot, dry sites. Shear plants back hard after flowering to prevent them from becoming bare in the centre.

'HidcoteBlue' lavender has a deep, rich colour. It is a favourite of professional landscapers. Fragro Plants photo

being stored under cover on a regular basis to ensure it has not gone too dry.

When you prune is also important for the survival of herbs, because pruning too early, before the growth season has begun, can seriously set back the plant. A light March pruning provides a perfect framework for the vigorous growth you can expect throughout the warmer months.

It's hard to give a general rule of thumb for how hard herbs should be pruned, as variables such as the age of the plant and variety in question are factors. I suggest that a little common sense and visual inspection could have you pruning accurately in most cases, as it is nearly impossible to err on the side of too much—unless you thought that pruning to ground level was appropriate.

I would like to comfort you with a loose guideline, though: your March pruning should leave the herb at a third to half of the size the herb grew to the previous summer. Ensure that every branch is pruned to this extent and your herb will be in good shape for the new season.

Q. *I would like to grow rosemary in my garden—what variety is the most cold hardy?*

A. When you are growing heat lovers like Mediterranean herbs, you are wise to choose a variety with the highest tolerance of cold. In this case, rosemary 'Arp' is the hardiest pick. In a severe winter, though, even it could die without some protection. Although 'Arp' is generally comfortable in zones 6* and warmer, you can improve its chances of surviving a notably icy winter by adding mulch or burlap over the root system. During extreme cold spells, consider draping the entire plant with burlap, removing it once all fear of freeze is gone. Or often people will grow rosemary in a container so that they can provide shelter November through March (see page 64).

See Natural Resources Canada's website, http://planthardiness.gc.ca, for Canada's current plant hardiness map.

Rosemary 'Arp' has a very upright form and is known as the most cold-hardy variety. There are many other varieties available, including a trailing form, Rosmarinus prostratus (zone 8).

SAGE

Q. *I often buy dried sage for cooking—is it easy to grow in the garden?*

A. Sage is very easy to grow. It prefers a sunny spot in the garden and is not overly particular about soil conditions. You can also have great success planting sage in containers. It grows extremely fast, and varieties such as 'Tri-Colour' are very attractive.

Harvesting regularly is advised to keep the plant in a firm, bushy form. To dry sage and many other herbs, bundle the stalks into a loose bouquet and place it upside down in a paper bag (crimping the top of the bag around the base of the upside-down clump). Hang the bag in a dark, cool room until the leaves have sufficiently dried, which can take anywhere from two weeks to a month, depending on the thickness of the leaves and temperature of the space.

Harvest sage in mid summer, when it will be of sufficient size following a spring pruning. This perennial herb requires a thorough and heavy pruning (to 8–12 in./20–30 cm from ground level) in March to prevent it from becoming too sprawling. Depending on the variety, sage can be quite vigorous. A thorough harvest in July—pruning off up to two-thirds of the new growth—will allow the plant to flush and produce a second crop to be gathered in September and beyond.

The benefits of sage are diverse, and I particularly like to make teas from the leaves, as they are not only tasty but help to soothe a sore throat for those of us who are a little chatty—or if we feel a cold coming on.

Sage can be grown in strawberry pots, along with other herbs. For a twist, try pineapple sage. It's great in cocktails.

Common sage (Salvia officinalis) is a good source of folic acid, thiamin and riboflavin.

BASIL

Q. *My basil never thrives—I plant it every spring and it just withers away and dies. Should I just give up?*

A. It is funny how often I hear people say, "I can't garden" or "I'm a plant killer." But when I delve a little more into it with them, they are not "bad gardeners" or "plant killers." Most often, it's simply the right plant in the wrong spot, environmental challenges or possibly not enough knowledge about care and maintenance of a particular plant. I guess the latter might make them a "plant killer," but we can easily work on that.

I can tell you with 100-percent certainty that what killed your basil was cold temperatures. Basil is a warm-climate plant that requires constant heat to thrive. Even if it warms up to a pleasant 68F (20C) during the day but cools off to 40–50F (5–10C) at night, your basil is going to die.

Basil is said to calm the nervous system and aid in digestion. Mostly, it tastes great on pizza!

So your basil challenge has got nothing to do with your abilities or deficiencies in gardening. A lack of continually warm temperatures is the sole problem.

I usually tell people not to bother planting basil outdoors until the end of May. Some think that if the weather is too cold for basil outdoors, the

Genovese basil (also called Italian large leaf basil) is the best variety to use for pesto or for colouring up a salad.

best solution is to keep it inside on a bright windowsill. Good thinking, but unfortunately that won't work either—the dry indoor environment will very quickly have basil deteriorating. So it's grocery-store basil for you until your planted-at-the-end-of-May basil is ready for harvest starting in about July.

But take heart—when basil does get going, it can grow like crazy. Before you know it, you've got bushes 2 ft. (60 cm) wide by 2 ft. (60 cm) tall.

So make sure you save some of that intense freshly harvested flavour for winter and the following spring when you're waiting to plant it again. Dry it or—even better—freeze it. Early in the morning, when the flavour within the basil leaf is at its peak, snip off about 30 large leaves. Slice them into smaller pieces and fill an ice-cube tray, then add water and freeze. Next, toss the frozen basil cubes into a plastic bag and store in your freezer. Come winter, whenever you are longing for the flavour of fresh-picked basil, simply pull out a few cubes and add them to your stews, soups and pasta sauces—or thaw and strain to complement mashed potatoes, hamburger patties or any recipe that could use an extra aromatic element.

DELICIOUS IDEAS…

Try some of the unique basil varieties such as 'Thai', 'Lemon', 'Spicy Globe', 'Dark Opal' (purple), 'Purple Ruffle' and more! That beloved basil flavour always dominates, but a hint of lemon or spice, or the stunning colour of 'Purple Ruffle', can add flavour and fun to pesto, salads and other favourites.

Purple ruffle basil (Ocimum basilicum purpurescens) has a slight clove scent. The colourful leaves make it a great accent plant in borders. Fragro Plants photo

GARLIC

Q. *When is the best time to plant garlic? I've seen it for sale at garden centres in both spring and fall, but I thought it was supposed to be planted in fall? And can I plant the garlic I buy from the grocery store?*

A. Good question, and a great way to sniff out an answer: garlic can be planted in spring, summer or fall. My preferences are fall and spring. Keep those crops coming!

Garlic can grow year round in many regions of the country, as it is very cold tolerant. Fall-planted garlic is harvested in late spring or summer, and the spring-planted crop is harvested in fall and winter.

Grocery-store garlic (and potatoes, for that matter) is not for planting in the garden. Often it's been sprayed with a retardant, and although they may start to sprout or send out shoots, the retardant will stunt growth.

Unlike some vegetables, garlic plants don't take up much space, so plant a lot of them. They keep for months after harvest.

Annuals

Annuals. It seems a shame. Why plant flowers that are going to die in a few short months? It is a little odd, don't you think?

However, in my opinion, not planting annuals would be like saying, "Let's skip summer this year." Yes, annuals only have a few months to live after planting—but their colour and scent can far surpass that of any perennial or shrub. We have many months when we're trapped indoors by inclement weather; when spring arrives, it's liberating to plant up our gardens and containers so that we can enjoy fragrant summer days. What's a Sunday-morning coffee or a midday mojito without that gorgeous colour all around us? It's what summer's all about!

Mother Nature makes it easy for us, too. If you want to put an assortment of different annuals in a container, all you really need to do is place the tall-growing ones in the centre, or toward the back, of a container or garden bed.

When it comes to fashion, you wouldn't wear a red sweater over an orange top, but colours in nature seem to blend without conflict. So go ahead and plant up some passionately purple heliotrope with bright-orange petunias and yellow tuberous begonias—and enjoy all the colours that annuals can bring to your yard, your patio and your life.

ANNUALS VERSUS PERENNIALS

What kind of balance should I be trying to achieve in my landscape between annuals and perennials?

Previous page: This urn of million bells (Calibrachoa) makes a bold statement. It is formal, classy and easy to create. You don't even have to plant it! Simply remove the wires and drop a million bells hanging basket into an urn. Proven Winners photo

The thought of having to plant only once—and to have those plants just get bigger and better every year—makes it easy to understand the attraction of perennials. As a result, perennials have become mainstream over the past decade, with a huge selection available.

The perennial category now offers so many different species and varieties, with a diversity of leaf and blossom colours and textures, heights and fragrances—to touch on just a few of the features in this gigantic category. Although perennials have a limited bloom time compared with annuals, there are varieties that bloom every single month of the year. Each one may only provide four to six weeks of bloom, but it adds up when you have a good mix with successive flowering times in your yard—moreover, many of today's perennials deliver huge blossom size, amazing colour and rich fragrance.

So why choose any annuals when perennials are apparently the be-all and end-all?

Oh wait, that was basically your question!

Annuals are typically a spring-through-fall category of plant, because come late fall or early winter, depending on when the frosts arrive, they are done. They die for two reasons—first, they have completed their life cycle of growing, blooming and setting or producing seed; second, for the most part, they can't tolerate cold, so the frost kills them.

Before I go into more detail, I should clarify that some of the plants we classify and use as annuals are actually perennials. Fuchsias and geraniums

These pink African daisies (Osteospermum) are very tolerant of cooler conditions. They are one of the first annuals that can be planted outdoors each spring.

are good examples. They do not fall under the perennial category and are usually referred to as annuals, because they can't tolerate the chilly temperatures and would simply die come winter frost. But if you can store these plants over winter in a cool frost-free room that won't get above 40F (5C), they can technically be classified as perennials. Dahlias, begonias and poinsettias are other examples of plants that could be considered annuals—or even disposables—in cool climates but in fact are perennial with a little TLC (read further into this section for more on this).

So, I won't complicate the topic further by telling you that there are both perennial and annual geraniums and fuchsias...but there are. I can see why some people get frustrated when trying to learn more about gardening.

Annuals serve their own important purpose that works very well in

unison with perennials in the garden. They can grow fast and furiously and for the most part bloom relatively soon—if not immediately—after planting. This offers quick coverage of large spaces to beautify a landscape. And, with just a few exceptions, annuals don't stop blooming until fall or early winter. So plant annuals in May to enjoy up to six months of colour in your garden. That's an easy win over the six weeks of blossoms offered by the average flowering perennial.

So there you have it—both annuals and perennials have different roles to play in the garden. I use both: perennials for back-of-the-garden structure

Bright cineraria (Senecio) liven up containers at front doors where they are protected from rain. They make up for not being the longest lasting annual by providing an array of vivid colours.

and annuals typically as fore-garden pick-me-ups to brighten borders and add spot colour throughout the summer. I think a 50/50 split would have your yard and garden bright and beautiful 12 months a year—though I would use a heavier emphasis on perennials for year-round "good bones."

WHAT TO PICK FOR A POT...

Annuals like residing in planters much more than perennials do. Annuals appreciate the extra heat a container environment gives their roots. Most perennials prefer growing in the cooler soil of an in-ground garden bed.

REVITALIZING HANGING BASKETS

Q.

Every April I purchase hanging baskets to decorate my townhome, but after three months or so, they don't look as fresh—is there something I can do to perk them up?

A. Beautiful, fresh hanging baskets bursting with colour are one of the most popular springtime garden treasures.

At our home, they are a highlight in our patio and porch areas, spring through summertime. But come mid to late July, they can look a little tired and spent.

That's when I pull out my hedge shears. With no concern for where or what I'm pruning off, I use those shears to clip away all the outer growth and blossoms, leaving each plant as just a green mound about half the size of its former self.

Talk about resilient—within two weeks, all the annuals in each hanging basket will have exploded in growth. Buds and blooms will replicate and even surpass their earlier glory. Don't forget to add fertilizer, though. After the trimming, the plant will need nutrition to ensure healthy, lush, green growth. Follow the feeding chart on page 147.

Let the shearing begin! This demonstration shows how to rein in an overgrown hanging basket (usually in mid summer).

Begin trimming with hedge shears, scissors or hand pruners.

The goal is to remove 50 percent of the growth, especially the long, trailing bits.

Don't forget to compost all clippings, as they're rich in nitrogen, which can warm and help compost the material in the box.

If you have a mixed basket with an upright plant in the centre, leave the centre plant alone. It's normally trailing plants that become leggy.

Although it appears drastic, this major cutback will benefit the basket in the long run. It will return to its original fullness in just two to three weeks.

Ten days later, back in bloom and ready to offer a compact flowering display through fall.

OVERWINTERING

> *How do I overwinter my annual geraniums? My mother keeps hers indoors on a windowsill, but they look scraggly come spring. And what about my fuchsias?*

Q.

A. Looks like I'm going to need to have a little chat with your mother. While she *is* overwintering her geraniums and keeping them alive, her method of doing this is not what's best for good, strong and healthy plants the following spring and summer. Based on how she is "storing them," she might even get some small blooms over the winter months inside the house—and again, this is not what we need in order to get the most from our geraniums the following year.

Geraniums need a dormant resting period, something not provided by residing on a windowsill inside a warm house through winter. With the toasty inside temperature but extremely low light level through the dark months, the geranium will stretch to reach for any possible light. Any of that growth will be spindly and weak. This is not the way that we want our geraniums to look as we approach spring.

To store your geraniums for winter, you'll need to dig them up from the

Above: *This variegated pink geranium can find winter accommodations in your garage or other cool but frost-free location until setting out the following spring.*
Left: *Multicoloured regal geraniums (Pelargonium) can be saved over from year to year. If you have a colour you particularly like, then it is worth the little effort to overwinter it.*

garden or outdoor containers in mid to late October, or prior to the first frost, and plant each one in a pot the size of its rootball. Usually a pot no deeper than 8 in. (20 cm) is necessary. If your geraniums are part of an outdoor container garden or planter, you have the choice of simply leaving them in the pots where they have been growing all summer and moving these containers to a cool location for storage—assuming they're not too heavy.

The beautiful 'Diva™ Bridal Pink' fuchsia is covered in delicate, soft-pink blossoms. Proven Winners photo

The best spot for them is in a cool but frost-free location; some light would be helpful but is not necessary if you can keep a relatively constant temperature of 34–40F (1–5C). Some locations that might work are a crawl space, an unused basement room, an enclosed garage or an outdoor shed that won't freeze. You could even place them in a box surrounded with packing or insulation material and keep this outside in an area protected from both rain and extreme cold. The latter method would work for temperate winter areas such as the Gulf Islands in British Columbia, for example.

Ensure you remove all dead and yellow leaves and debris from the plant or soil and even prune them back by about a third prior to tucking them away for the winter. Excess size and an abundance of leaves can be a hindrance to overwintering plants, as they're simply too much for the dormant geranium to support.

You may still need to check them to ensure that the soil they reside in over winter doesn't go too dry. Although they aren't in need of much water, you don't want the plant dehydrating to the point of no return either.

The popular summer-blooming fuchsias can be overwintered in the exact same fashion.

TIME TO WAKE UP!

Come late February, it's time for those geraniums and fuchsias to wake up.

The first task is to clean them up. Pull off any dead or browning leaves and prune the plants down by one-third of their height. This is after your relatively hard pruning in the fall, so this pruning will bring the plant down to about half the size it was at the time of digging it up in the fall. You may end up without a leaf in sight, but the plants will start sending out new shoots very shortly after pruning.

Next, place the plants where there is as much light as possible. A nice, bright window would be great, but not in a room that's too warm. A cool garage window or a bright, cool

basement window would be ideal. Got a greenhouse? If you do, you can start waking up your plants in early February. What's key at this point is that your geraniums and fuchsias still need a cool environment. If it's too warm, they'll stretch for light and the new growth will be gangly. Food is also important at this stage, and providing your plants with fish fertilizer at half-strength every two weeks will get them well on their way to a bloom-filled summer. Place them outdoors in your flower beds or containers after the middle of May.

Left: Red is still the most popular colour of geranuim, outselling the others by three to one!

How can I get begonias growing in time to use them all summer to fill my patio planters and hanging baskets?

Starting begonia tubers (bulbs) indoors in March is extremely easy and very rewarding. The biggest and best begonias come from tubers planted in February/March. Plant each tuber in lightweight potting soil in its own 4-in. (10-cm) pot at soil level—so that the tuber is just barely showing at the top of the pot. And always plant with the hollow on the top of the tuber facing up.

Place the pots on the sill of a bright window and water to keep each tuber slightly moist. Once the new shoots grow to 4 in. (10 cm), you'll want to get them to a cooler spot (40–50F/5–10C); otherwise, they'll start stretching as they hunt for more light, which is simply not available in the low-light month of March.

Keep them inside in the cool location, where they'll continue to develop

Above: This single-flowered fuchsia is definitely worth trying to save over from year to year.
Proven Winners photo

Starting your begonias from tubers (bulbs) is the best way to get a head start on the growing season. An added bonus is that many colours and varieties are only available in the tuber form.

in a slow and compact fashion and fill the pot with roots, until you can plant them outside once all danger of frosts are gone for the spring. You can also tuck them into hanging baskets and containers, but again, be mindful of cold temperatures if you're placing them directly outdoors.

DAHLIAS

How should I plant and care for dahlias to get the biggest, boldest blooms possible?

A. There are few people, even non-gardeners, who aren't familiar with the glorious flowers of dahlias. Easily the most popular summer-blooming flowering tuber/bulb among commercial growers and gardeners alike, their beauty, vigour and easy care make them great value for the gardening dollar. Still, you don't see them in that many gardens, which indicates there is much more potential for them. Once they try them, most people are hooked on dahlias and will want to experiment with more of the numerous unique types and new varieties introduced every year.

Although I emphasize easy care, there are a few things you should know about rearing and maintaining dahlias. My initial experience with them was many years ago in the small garden of my first home. Like so many new dahlia growers, my mistake was not providing these plants with enough room to grow without smothering all other life forms in their vicinity.

It's important to know that there are more than 2,000 varieties of dahlias available—and depending on which ones you choose, they can mature to a height anywhere from 1–10 ft. (30 cm–3 m). And, as a general rule, most dahlia varieties reach a width of at least 50 percent of their mature height. So, when selecting dahlias, be sure to check out the height and width they will grow to, so that you can ensure there is enough space in your flower beds.

Otherwise, dahlias are quite low maintenance and easy to grow. With the exception of some of the smaller border varieties, they're best grown in full sun directly out in your flower beds. Smaller varieties may be grown in containers.

Taller-growing dahlias look exceptional at the back of a flower bed or up against a south-facing fence or wall, where they add depth and colour. The flowers themselves tend to face the sun, so planting them in full sun in a northern or eastern area of your yard will assure you the greatest visibility of blossoms from your house.

Dahlias date back to the 1500s in Mexico and were favoured by the Aztecs. There are so many varieties to choose from. Your local garden centre will have a great selection in March.

Although dahlia tubers are generally planted earlier in the season, there is still time in late May and early June to get them going. When planting tubers, I normally like to dig the hole to at least twice the planting depth (approximately 20 in./50 cm) and fill the base of the planting hole with a combination of compost, mushroom manure and coir (coco-fibre material) or peat moss. The site should have good drainage, but the planting medium must retain a certain amount of moisture to support the massive amount of foliage produced by most dahlia varieties. I also recommend mixing 1 lb. (500 g) of a low-nitrogen, slow-release granular fertilizer (such as 8-20-20) into 2 cu. ft. (56 L) of the planting medium—That's about 2 cups (500 mL) of fertilizer mixed into a small wheelbarrow filled with soil.

No matter how much time you have, or do not have, for care and maintenance of your dahlias throughout the growing season, you'll likely experience success. However, one procedure I definitely recommend is the removal of a few of the young shoots shortly after they have emerged from the soil, simply by pinching them out with thumb and forefinger. By limiting the quantity of shoots a dahlia tuber produces to 7–10, you will maximize the quality and, believe it or not, quantity of blooms from each plant by season's end.

And if your preference is for a full and bushy plant, you can achieve this by pinching off just the tips of those remaining 7–10 emerging shoots after they've grown to a height of approximately 8–10 in. (20–25 cm).

One other maintenance issue that is integral to growing dahlias is staking the plants. Gardeners sometimes use a tomato cage as a support system. This works well for medium-height choices, but for taller-growing varieties, it's best to combine the tomato cage with a number of 6-ft. (1.8-m) wooden or bamboo garden stakes to which you can affix the major dahlia stalks. For

Imagine this bloom as a cut flower in a vase on your kitchen table—right from your own backyard.

best results and the least potential for tuber damage, position your support structure of stakes and/or tomato cage immediately after planting each tuber. As the stalks grow, loosely adhere them to the stake using a vinyl tie, which is a stretchy material that won't cut into the stem. Vinyl tie is available at your local garden centre and usually comes on a 165-ft. (50-m) roll.

Dahlias, like all plants, can experience the occasional pest problem. Aphids favour dahlias; however, if you notice an infestation early enough, you can control it by washing away the insects with a steady stream from a garden hose. For bad infestations, turn to page 217. Weevils, too, sometimes leave telltale holes in dahlia leaves. Unless the problem is severe, I generally let them be, as the damage is more aesthetic than it is harmful to the plant.

Dahlias should be given a deep watering once a week—approximately half an hour of water application will do if the plants are rooted in a good soil mix. Overhead sprinkling is not advised, so use a low-height sprinkler or irrigation system, or simply place a hose near the base of the plant. Direct watering with a hose will reduce the amount of required watering time to about 15 minutes. Move the running hose two or three times over the 15 minutes to ensure that you thoroughly water the entire root zone, about a 4-ft. (120-cm) radius from the base of the plant.

They also benefit from a feeding every two weeks, using a water-soluble flowering-plant fertilizer mixed at the recommended strength.

As your dahlia specimens bloom, be sure to pinch off the finished flowers, or "deadhead," to encourage additional blooming from the plant. And, as an added bonus, cutting blossoms for indoor enjoyment will further force bud set. So make a point of savouring a few of those large, luscious dahlia blooms indoors in a vase—they create a wonderful bouquet and are quite long-lived as cut flowers.

Some varieties of dahlias have blooms up to 1 ft. (30 cm) wide.

DISBUDDING TO OPTIMIZE BLOOMS

As the season progresses and your ultimate goal of large blossoms looks imminent, you may want to remove a few of those flower buds. Three flower buds will develop at each leaf axil, and periodically pinching out one or two of the three will encourage the remaining flowers to be larger, with longer stems. This process is known as disbudding and is often practised by exhibition growers.

Tip: Keep each dahlia bulb in its original package until you're ready to plant, as all tubers look the same, and you wouldn't want to plant the shorter growing varieties where you wanted the taller growing varieties, or vice versa.

How do I store my dahlias over winter?

A. Not only are dahlias great performers the very first season, but they actually can get bigger and better over their first few years. The only drawback to the dahlia is that it is not a winter-hardy plant, so each tuber (the equivalent of a bulb), needs to be dug up and stored over the cold months. The process, however, is quite simple:

Tip: Do you love tuberous begonias, gladiolas and canna lilies? Store them over the winter just as you would dahlia tubers.

1. After the first frost of fall or winter, you'll notice that the tops or upper part of the dahlia greens will turn brown. They have been burned by the frost. This is the time to dig them up. Gently lift the tubers from the earth by using a garden fork, lightly pulling the stalk at the same time. You want to take extreme care inserting the fork into the soil and lifting the tubers, as the slightest cut or bruising of a tuber's protective outer skin will create a spot vulnerable to rot in the forthcoming winter-storage period.

2. Once you have the tuber out of the ground, shake off the majority of the earth and cut the tops to about 6 in. (15 cm) from the tubers themselves. Don't forget that the upper portion you removed from each tuber is great composting material.

3. Now move the tubers to a dry, cool location and set them on some newspaper to dry for approximately 24 to 72 hours. The excess soil on the tuber should dry so that you can easily brush it off.

4. At this point, they're ready to be placed in their sleeping quarters. Find a sturdy cardboard box big enough to house all your tubers, and then add about 4–6 in. (10–15 cm) of dry sand, sawdust or peat moss to the bottom. Place each tuber upside down (to ensure any moisture from the stalks wicks away from the tuber) and at least 2 in. (5 cm) apart from each other. Clearly mark the variety or colour but ensure you don't attach anything to the tuber; instead, use a twist tie or an elastic band to attach a label to the stalk.

5. When you've filled the bottom layer, add another 4–6-in. (10–15-cm) layer of the medium and another layer of tubers. Keep doing this until the box is full, assuming you have that many tubers to store.

6. You can close the box up, but cut four holes approximately 2 × 2 in. (5 × 5 cm) in size in the top corners to allow any moisture within to escape. Now find a cool room, closet or enclosed garage to store the box. A constant temperature that is above freezing but below 50F (10C) is preferred. They will remain here until ready for planting the following April, when they'll outperform the previous year's blooms.

These are examples of the variety in dahlia bloom shape and colour. Mature heights also vary greatly, so you could easily fill a huge flower bed with only dahlias and have a fabulous show of shorter varieties up front with towering eight-footers in the back! *NFBIC photos*

Left to right, top to bottom: *Dahlia 'Toyama'; Dahlia 'Akita'; Dahlia 'Osaka'; Dahlia 'Amante'; and Dahlia 'Alfred Grille'*

FORCING BULBS

Q. *I see spring-blooming bulbs in flower in winter—how do I do this?*

A. There are a few varieties of traditionally spring-blooming outdoor bulbs that can undergo a process where they are "prepared." This is where growers take the bulbs and chill them for 6–12 weeks, depending on species, through late summer and fall to the extent that the cold period mimics a winter as far as the bulb is concerned. This process is called "forcing." Quite appropriate.

Next, following the enforced cold spell, the bulb is planted into an indoor container in October, November or December, where it will quickly send out a flower bud and likely bloom within a month. it's a great way to have a little bit of spring indoors during the dreary months of winter.

Crocus blooms bursting open in February herald the imminent arrival of spring. These bulbs are always good value, as they naturalize readily.

There's no reason why you can't do this, too. The most common bulbs that are forced are tulips and hyacinths; however, this process can also be extended to narcissus and crocus. Simply put your bulbs into a cold-storage space—the meat compartment of your fridge works well—and leave them there for a minimum of six weeks. Store some longer if you want to plant up a few every week in order to extend the length of time you will have blooming bulbs on display inside your home. Typically, they can take up to a month to bloom after they are planted and given the warmth of your home.

Some varieties work better than others, so check with your local garden centre in early fall for their selection of bulbs suitable for forcing.

Left: Choose bulbs with different blooming heights for a better display. *NFBIC photo*

Middle: Deep-purple hyacinths in a decorative vessel, underplanted with black mondo grass for a dramatic effect. *NFBIC photo*

AMARYLLIS

How do I get my amaryllis to re-bloom the following year?

A. Without a doubt, amaryllis is the king…or queen…of bulbs. Having festive lily-like blooms in one of many colours, spanning 6–8 in. (15–20 cm) or more atop a stalk of 2–3 ft. (60–90 cm), inside your home during the holiday season pretty much says it all.

On top of that, they're easy to grow and, purchased as a bulb in the fall at your local garden centre, results are guaranteed. Simply plant the bulb in a 6–8-in. (15–20-cm) container, and then set it in a nice bright spot in your home to watch it grow. The stalk and flower bud is the first part to emerge, with leaves following when blooming has finished.

Okay, January has arrived and the holiday is over. Your amaryllis looks as green as Uncle Tony did after someone thought it wise to bring out the home-made grappa. Now it's time to find a cool, bright spot for your plant—and it

Top right: An assortment of bulbs suitable for forcing: tulips, hyacinths and muscari. Packages will identify whether a bulb variety can be forced. *NFBIC photo*

Amaryllis (Hippeastrum ssp.) are native to South America. This is a stunning example of their beauty! NFBIC photo

WHEN BULBS
ARE BEST
Amaryllis is available in dozens of different varieties and colours but usually only when purchased as a bulb in fall as opposed to a pre-grown bloom handled by a grower. Growers will usually take the safe route, planting only the most popular varieties.

needs to remain indoors until the weather has warmed to the point where there is no fear of frost. This will likely be sometime in May.

Find a nice bright, sheltered spot to plant it in your garden. Although amaryllis can tolerate sun, if you don't have a suitable location to plant it right into your garden and need to keep it potted, I suggest you locate it where it won't be subject to the afternoon sun.

The next phase for an amaryllis is plant development and bud set, which is best achieved in an outdoor environment. And, to further assist it, whether it is in a pot or in the ground, I recommend feeding it on a weekly basis with a liquid organic flowering-plant fertilizer.

So, as you relax and enjoy some fresh air and sunshine over the summer, so should your amaryllis plant until…dun, dun, dun…late August. This is when the vacation is over.

Take the bulb out of the pot or ground by grabbing it at the base of all of its leaves and tugging it out. It should pull out relatively easily, but you might need to wiggle it a little bit. The bulb, that is. Shake off the majority of the earth and then cut off all the leaves to about 3 in. (7.5 cm) from the top of the bulb. Although this sounds harsh, it's necessary.

You now need to find a cool (40–50F/5–10C), dark spot to store the bulb on top of some newspaper for about six to eight weeks. Basically, you will be faking winter, albeit a warm winter. After this period of dormancy, begin the process over again by planting the bulb and watching the stalk and flower bud grow until showtime.

TIPS TO OPTIMIZE YOUR AMARYLLIS BLOOM OVER THE HOLIDAY SEASON

1. As the flower bud begins its ascent toward your ceiling, turn the pot to ensure the stalk doesn't start reaching for the light from a window, giving you the Leaning Tower of Amaryllis. A quarter rotation daily is not enough to make the plant dizzy but sufficient to keep it growing straight.

2. If the stalk seems to be growing too fast and you were hoping to have the bloom as the centrepiece for Christmas dinner, slow it down by placing it in a cool room. Assuming there is good light, you can keep it there for as long as you wish. You can move it in and out of the cool location as many times as needed to regulate the growth to meet your bloom time schedule. Your guests will be amazed at how you orchestrated the blooms perfectly to be enjoyed at your celebration.

3. You can also extend the life of the bloom by placing the plant in a cooler spot every night. A cool basement room, an enclosed garage or even below a sheltering overhang outdoors will suffice as long as temperatures don't dip below freezing.

Like geraniums, red is the most popular colour for amaryllis. This 'Red Lion' is the variety chosen most often. NFBIC photo

POINSETTIAS

Q. *At the beginning of last December, a friend gave me a poinsettia plant. Although the holiday season has passed, it has hardly lost any of its leaves and looks very healthy. What is the annual care and maintenance required so that it will bloom for me next year?*

What colour of poinsettia is the biggest seller? You guessed it: red!

A. Many people regard the poinsettia as a special addition to their festive decorating. No other plant better represents the warmth and appeal of the holiday season.

But it need not end there—there is a way to enjoy poinsettias year round, without losing the particular appeal they have in the holidays. After you have enjoyed the plant through December and January, remove any remaining bracts (the coloured part that we refer to as the flowers). Keep it inside as an attractive leafy houseplant, but find a cool spot to ensure its survival through May.

Now comes the drastic part: in late May, cut the plant's height down by half and place it in the garden or on your patio in a filtered-light environment. This would also be a good time to repot it. And it's important to fertilize it biweekly with 20-20-20.

Keep your poinsettia outside until mid August, then bring it indoors and start giving it long, long nights—we're talking 16 hours of darkness every day—by keeping it in a closet or dark room, wherever there is total darkness without natural or artificial light. This can be a little monotonous, but it will ensure the bracts colour up. During this process, keep the plant moist and protect it from any hot or cold drafts.

After about 45 days, or when you notice the plant is getting the poinsettia's true colour—full bract formation is not necessary, but the plant must have begun its colour process—move the poinsettia to exactly where you want to display it for the remainder of the holiday season. Then…repeat step one.

This 'Marble' poinsettia was created by crossing a pink and a white poinsettia.

Perennials

Perennials

Perennials are one of the fastest-growing categories in garden centres over the past decade, morphing from a few obscure plants relegated to the back of the greenhouse to a wide selection displayed front and centre with annuals.

The fact that perennial plants come back year after year is clearly their most prized attribute; however, it doesn't hurt that breeders are improving varieties all the time to make them more compact and urban-garden friendly, with better flower quality and unique leaf colours. Perennials also extend the window of interest in a garden with variations that include winter bloomers and increasingly come in varying shapes and sizes, including tall-growing cultivars to fill the back areas of flower beds.

Today, older perennials like black-eyed Susans (Rudbeckia) and coral bells (*Heuchera*) have all kinds of cultivars available in each group, thanks to the efforts of dedicated plant breeders. Coneflowers (Echinacea) are now available in doubles, singles, whites, oranges and yellows. The lowly hosta family has literally exploded with new varieties from tiny, dwarf types (*Hosta* 'Blue Mouse', growing to only 7 inches) to huge leafy types (*Hosta* 'Blue Umbrellas', growing to 40 inches).

With a wide assortment of perennials to choose from, there is a plant for every purpose. Commercial landscapers are using perennials much more freely than before. Large beds around strip malls and apartment buildings are now being filled with helleborus (Christmas rose) and *hostas, heucheras* and *hemerocallis* (daylilies). Municipalities are filling medians with ornamental grasses and evergreen perennials. In residential applications, people are adding perennials to shady, small or dry areas.

From an environmental standpoint, perennials have a much smaller carbon footprint than annuals. This is because, in the growing process, they do not have the energy requirements (heated greenhouses) that bedding plants do. They also have lower fertilizer requirements in this stage. Economically, they are a better investment than bedding plants as they can live and be enjoyed for many years.

BEYOND TULIPS AND DAFFS

Although tulips and daffodils are by far the most commonly grown spring-blooming bulbs, don't hesitate to try some of the other amazing choices, such as fritillaria or allium, which can offer greater heights and unique blossoms and are just as easy to grow.

Previous page: I can only imagine the fragrance I would smell walking down this path lined with tulip and narcissus. It's also quick and easy access for snipping a few blossoms for an indoor vase.

Just Ask *Wim!*

YEAR-ROUND COLOUR

Right now it seems like I have a lot of spring colour but not much through the rest of the year—what plants can I add so that I have year-round colour in my yard?

Q.

A. Perennials are a wonderful opportunity to enjoy beautiful colour in the garden right through the year. Remember to position plants with winter interest where you can enjoy seeing them from inside your home on a chilly fall or winter day.

Here are some of my favourite plants for 12 months of colour, and remember that stopping by your garden centre throughout the year will give you even more ideas for your landscape through spring, summer, fall and winter:

12 Months of Perennial Colour

F – Flower | CL – Colourful Leaf

The zones indicated in this book are the minimum hardiness zones per genus. Individual cultivar hardiness zones could vary. Check with your local nursery for clarification.

JANUARY
- **Christmas rose (F)**, *Helleborus* – zone 4
- **Pigsqueak (CL)**, *Bergenia* – zone 5

FEBRUARY
- **Coral bells (CL)**, *Heuchera* – zone 5
- **Hardy cyclamen (F)**, *Cyclamen hederifolium* – zone 6

MARCH
- **Evergreen spurge (F)**, *Euphorbia wulfenii* '**Shorty**' – zone 7
- **Lungwort (CL)**, *Pulmonaria saccharata* – zone 5
- **Purple sage (CL)**, *Salvia officinalis* '**Purpurascens**' – zone 5

APRIL
- **Aubretia (F)**, *Aubretia* – zone 4
- **Bleeding heart (F)**, *Dicentra spectabilis* – zone 3
- **Marsh marigold (F)**, *Caltha palustris* – zone 3
- **Siberian bugloss (F), (CL)**, *Brunnera macrophylla* 'Jack Frost' – zone 3
- **Wallflower (F)**, *Erysimum* '**Bowles Mauve**' – zone 6

Top, euphorbia; ***bottom***, *bleeding heart.*

Perennials

MAY
- Calla lily (F), *Zantedeschia aethiopica* – zone 6
- Garden pinks (F), *Dianthus* 'Neon Star' – zone 4
- Oriental poppy (F), *Papaver orientale* – zone 3
- Peony (F), *Paeonia* – zone 3
- Sweet William (F), *Dianthus barbatus* – zone 3

JUNE
- Blue lithospermum (F), *Lithodora diffusa* 'Grace Ward' – zone 5
- Delphinium (F), *Delphinium elatum* – zone 3
- False spirea (F), *Astilbe* – zone 4
- Lavender (F), *Lavandula angustifolia* – zone 5
- Rock soapwort (F), *Saponaria ocymoides* – zone 4
- Serbian bellflower (F), *Campanula poscharskyana* 'Blue Waterfall' – zone 4

JULY
- Bee balm (F), *Monarda* 'Jacob Cline' – zone 4
- Blazing stars (F), *Liatrus spicata* – zone 3
- Coneflower (F), *Echinacea purpurea* – zone 4
- Daylily (F), *Hemerocallis* 'Stella de Oro' – zone 3
- Garden phlox (F), *Phlox paniculata* – zone 4
- Hosta (F), (CL), *Hosta* – zone 3

Glorious, fragrant perennial lilies are guaranteed performers, with very little annual maintenance. NFBIC photo

AUGUST
- Blanket flower (F), *Gaillardia* × *grandiflora* – zone 2
- Cranesbill (F) *Geranium* 'Rozanne' – zone 5
- Japanese windflower (F), *Anemone* 'September Charm' – zone 5
- Monkshood (F), *Aconitum napellus* – zone 3
- Oriental lilies (F), *Lilium* – zone 3
- Red hot poker (F), *Kniphofia uvaria* – zone 5

SEPTEMBER
- Balloon flower (F), *Platycodon* – zone 4
- Black-eyed Susan (F), *Rudbeckia* – zone 3
- Globe thistle (F), *Echinops rifro* – zone 5
- Sneezeweed (F), *Helenium* 'Mardi Gras' – zone 4
- Tickseed (F), *Coreopsis* species – zone 4

OCTOBER
- Aster (F), *Aster* – zone 4
- Fall mum (F), *Chrysanthemum* – zone 5
- Showy stonecrop (F), *Sedum* 'Autumn Joy' – zone 4

NOVEMBER
- **Bugleweed (CL),** *Ajuga reptans* – zone 3
- **Foamflower (CL),** *Tiarella cordifolia* – zone 4
- **Ivy (CL),** *Hedera helix* 'Goldheart' – zone 5

DECEMBER
- **Blue fescue (CL),** *Festuca glauca* 'Elijah Blue' – zone 4
- **Blue oat grass (CL),** *Helictotrichon sempervirens* – zone 5
- **Hens and chicks (CL),** *Sempervivum tectorum* – zone 4

12 Months of Landscape Colour

F – Flower | S – Shrub | V – Vine | T – Tree | B – Bulb

JANUARY
- **Himalayan sweetbox (S),** *Sarcoccoca hookeriana* var. *humilis* – zone 6
- **Snowdrops (B),** *Galanthus nivalis* – zone 3
- **Witch hazel (S),** *Hamamelis vernalis* – zone 5
- **Winter aconite (B),** *Eranthis hyemalis* – zone 4

FEBRUARY
- **Christmas rose (F),** *Helleborus* – zone 4
- **Heather (F),** *Erica carnea* – zone 4
- **Winter jasmine (V),** *Jasminium nudiflorum* – zone 6
- **Camellia (S),** *Camellia japonica* – zone 7

MARCH
- **Cornelian cherry dogwood (T),** *Cornus mas* – zone 4
- **English daisy (F),** *Bellis perennis* – zone 4
- **Forsythia (S),** *Forsythia* × *intermedia* – zone 5
- **PJM rhododendron (S),** *Rhododendron* 'PJM' – zone 4
- **Star magnolia (T),** *Magnolia stellata* – zone 5

APRIL
- **Candytuft (F),** *Iberis sempervirens* – zone 3
- **Cushion spurge (F),** *Euphorbia polychroma* – zone 5
- **Flowering currant (S),** *Ribes sanguineum* – zone 5
- **Flowering dogwood (T),** *Cornus florida* – zone 5
- **Flowering quince (S),** *Chaenomeles japonica* – zone 5
- **Redbud (T),** *Cersis canadensis* – zone 5

Hen and chicks (Sempervivum) is an incredibly low-maintenance and drought-tolerant plant that is great for rockeries, gardens, planters or even wall planters. NFBIC photo

A West Coast classic, the rhododendron remains a favourite for its durability and performance. It actually enjoys rain and overcast skies!

SHOW TIME
Many perennials grow very well in containers—choose hardy non-herbaceous varieties for the best year-round display.

MAY

- **Flowering cherry (T),** *Prunus subhirtella* – zone 5
- **Golden chain tree (T),** *Laburnum anagyroides* – zone 5
- **Kerria (S),** *Kerria japonica* – zone 4
- **Peony (F),** *Paeonia* – zone 3
- **Rhododendron (S),** *Rhododendron* – zone 6
- **Wisteria (V),** *Wisteria floribunda* – zone 5

JUNE

- **California lilac (S),** *Ceanothus thyrsiflorus* – zone 7
- **Clematis (V),** *Clematis montana* – zone 6
- **Japanese snowbell (T),** *Styrax japonicus* – zone 5
- **Mock orange (S),** *Philadelphus lewisii* – zone 5
- **Snowmound spirea (S),** *Spiraea nipponica* **'Snowmound'** – zone 4
- **Roses (S),** *Rosa* – zone 3 and up

JULY

- **Beard tongue (F),** *Penstemon* – zone 3
- **Evergreen magnolia (T),** *Magnolia grandiflora* – zone 7
- **Maltese cross (F),** *Lychnis chalcedonica* – zone 3
- **Queen of the prairie (F),** *Filipendula rubra* – zone 3

AUGUST

- **Crocosmia (B),** *Crocosmia* '**Lucifer'** – zone 5
- **Dahlia (B),** *Dahlia* – zone 8
- **Joe pye weed (F),** *Eupatorium purpureum* – zone 5
- **Hydrangea (S),** *Hydrangea macrophylla* – zone 6
- **Rose of Sharon (S),** *Hibiscus syriacus* – zone 6

SEPTEMBER

- **Aster (F),** *Aster* – zone 4
- **Black-eyed Susan (F),** *Rudbeckia* – zone 3
- **Boston ivy (V),** *Parthenocissus tricuspidata* – zone 5
- **Fall mum (F),** *Chrysanthemum* – zone 5
- **Showy stonecrop (F),** *Sedum* '**Autumn Joy'** – zone 4

OCTOBER

- **Japanese maples (T),** *Acer palmatum* **ssp.** – zone 6
- **Ornamental kale (F),** *Brassica oleracea* – zone 6
- **Winter pansies (F),** *Viola* × *wittrockiana* – zone 4

NOVEMBER

- **Beautyberry (S),** *Callicarpa bodinieri* – zone 6
- **Holly (S),** *Ilex* × *meserveae* – zone 5
- **Silver Korean fir (T),** *Abies koreana* '**Horstmann's Silberlocke'** – zone 5

DECEMBER

- **Coral bark maple (T),** *Acer palmatum* '**Sango-kaku'** – zone 5
- **Red twig dogwood (S),** *Cornus stolonifera* – zone 4
- **Viburnum (S),** *Viburnum* × *bodnantense* '**Dawn'** – zone 5

TOP TIP

One of the greatest things you can do for your garden is to top-dress your beds once every year or two. The addition of soil, mulch or manure helps to protect from winter cold or summer drought and offers additional growing medium for your plants.

Hollies have three things going for them: they are evergreen, they are hardy and they have bright-red berries for winter interest. And of, course, you can always cut your own fresh holly sprigs at Christmas.

SINKING SOIL

Two years ago, I built a raised bed and filled it with "garden blend" soil. Starting last year, the soil level began to sink. I could just top it up, but I have quite a few perennials in the bed now and I'm afraid of burying them too deeply. What should I do?

A. Whether in a raised or ground-level bed, compost and soil will decompose into smaller particles, shrinking the volume and producing what I like to call "sinking-bed syndrome." Rain and snow can also cause compaction, which further lowers the soil level.

You will need to top up the raised bed with more garden soil. To ensure your perennials aren't buried too deep, simply lift them to the new level in spring or fall, using a spading fork. Push your fork all around the perimeter of each perennial, gently loosening it by prying the fork farther back with each insertion into the soil.

Next, and ideally with two people who are both armed with spading forks and prying from opposite sides of the perennial, raise the root system by simultaneously pulling both forks backwards when the tines are deep below the root system. This will lift the plant, allowing you to place enough soil below the roots to position the clump at the desired height. If you only need to add an inch or two of soil, then you will be able to do so without having to hoist the clump right out.

A dry-stack wall helps showcase a mixed perennial bed.

TUBERS AND BULBS

Do tubers and bulbs require a high-phosphorus fertilizer for their spring growth?

Q.

A. Tubers and bulbs do require a higher-phosphorous fertilizer than most perennials and annuals.

The placement of this fertilizer is also important. Bulbs and tubers like to grow a healthy root system below the bulb or tuber itself. Gardeners are often generous with good soil and fertilizer above the bulb or tuber; however, gravel could also be put there, for that matter, as the bulb or tuber will push growth through pretty much any material overhead. The most important placement of good soil and fertilizer is 4–6 in. (10–15 cm) below the bulb.

And now that you know where to put it, your best bet for high-phosphorous nutrition for any bulb or tuber is bone meal mixed thoroughly into the earth. For more on this, check out our next question.

The double blooms of the ranunculus make this a beautiful cut flower. Outside, they look best in containers protected from rainfall. They are available in bulb and potted form in early spring.

Top: *This purple calla lily (Zantedeschia) can grow to a height of approximately 16 in. (40 cm), it is useful in containers and mixed borders.*
Bottom: *Gardeners have used bone meal for a long time, and it remains the best food for these bulbs! NFBIC photo*

Q. *My tulips seem stunted—they don't grow tall, and the flower is not as large as what I see in other gardens. What am I doing wrong?*

A. Although it is quite possible that it is something you're doing wrong, don't feel bad— it's a relatively common problem.

Newly purchased bulbs have everything they need to perform in your garden the following spring. Fertilizing and proper planting achieve long-term fantastic results for future years. And one of the great things about bulbs is that they generally do last for years if they're planted correctly. Some bulbs even naturalize and, in addition to blooming every year, spread to create more spring beauty with little effort on your part.

As addressed in our previous question, the common mistake people make when planting bulbs is that they provide great loose earth *on top* of the bulb.

If you dig a hole to the required depth but don't work the earth below, the bulb will have a difficult time rooting out into the earth. The consequences can be a stunted growth and most likely smaller leaves and flowers, along with a bulb that is unable to replenish the following year.

Consider adding at least 4 in. (10 cm) of good soil below a bulb or tuber when planting—and even up to 8 in. (20 cm) for larger bulbs such as fritillaria. This will, without a doubt, offer you the best results in both the short and long term. Use a good mixture of a very porous soil, which could include a combination of sand, compost, bark mulch and soil,

Despite the staggering number of tulip varieties available today, the traditional-looking tulips will always put on a good show.

with a healthy amount of bone meal mixed in. Because I recommend planting smaller bulbs in clusters of five, I suggest a minimum soil base of a shovelful (2–3 L) of any combination of the above amendments, along with ¼ cup (60 mL) of bone meal, mixed in with a similar amount of the existing soil.

Planted well, bulbs should provide you with a carefree and very rewarding boost of late-winter/early-spring colour and fragrance to brighten both your garden and your spirits.

Q.

I purchased some spring-blooming bulbs in fall and then set them aside and forgot about them. It's December—should I plant them now or wait until next year?

A. As you know, spring-blooming bulbs—such as daffodils, tulips, crocuses and hyacinths—need to be planted in the fall. This allows them to grow a healthy root system that will support the emerging flower bud and leaves the following spring. Planting them September through November is the ultimate, as the soil still has some warmth to it from the summer months and this encourages root growth.

So what happens if the bulb is not planted during that period? If it's not in the ground, it will start to dehydrate. Having said that, I recall a cool December day of rummaging through my garage and coming across my own forgotten bag of bulbs, brought home on a September evening with every noble intention of planting them that very weekend. Oops. But, hey, these things happen.

__Left__: Dig a hole for planting tulips, then incorporate bone meal into the bottom of the hole. Jay Shaw photo
__Right, top to bottom__: "11,12,13… drat! Lost count." No worries. When you plant in a cluster, there is no need to ensure there is an odd or even number. Always plant bulbs with the pointed end facing up. Try to avoid planting in straight lines or rows. Backfill the planting hole gently but firmly. Finish by watering the area well. Dig, drop, done! Jay Shaw photos

Nevertheless, it is amazing how long a bulb can last out of soil, as I have planted them as late as January and they each still managed to throw out a flower that spring. Although the blossoms were not what they could have been, I did save the bulbs for future years.

Not planting until January, though, would mean a bulb has been out of soil for five to six months, which would definitely start to compromise its integrity. Nevertheless, whenever you happen to discover that bag of bulbs in the garage, the best strategy is to get them in the ground as quickly as possible, planting them as you normally would have in the fall months.

Okay, enough talking…time to get those bulbs in the ground!

BUT ARE THE BULBS STILL WORTH PLANTING?

If you doubt the viability of the bulbs and want to check them before you go to the bother of planting, there is a simple test. Squeeze each bulb firmly at its widest diameter between your thumb and forefinger, slightly rotating your fingers to check that the bulb is firm. If it is, this likely means there is still enough moisture inside the bulb to start it growing after planting. If it's soft, it has begun to rot within and will not grow; if it completely breaks apart, it has dehydrated—in either case, it is best destined for the compost box.

Large, plump and firm bulbs will offer you the best show.
NFBIC photo

My tulips are almost finished blooming—how quickly can I cut their foliage back?

A. All bulbs—tulip, daffodil, crocus, hyacinth and all of the specialty varieties available—need to replenish their energy so the timing of when you cut the foliage off will impact bulb quality.

Your first step—once each bulb's flower petals fall—is to remove the seed head left behind. A bulb expends significant energy to bring seeds to maturity, but for most of us weekend gardeners, this serves no purpose, since we don't need or want seeds from our bulbs. The removal of the pod will then send the bulb into its final stage prior to dormancy, which is the storing up of nutrition.

Next, the bulb will absorb any nourishment left within the remaining leaves. The leaves are rich in nutrients needed to fuel the development of next spring's flower bud and leaves, including nitrogen, phosphorus and potash, along with trace elements essential to the bulb's good health. Even if you fed the bulbs with fertilizer to supplement the nutrition lost by cutting the leaves off prematurely, it would not be enough or as accessible to the bulb, and its bloom would not be optimum the following year. So leave the foliage on those tulips or any other bulb at least until it has yellowed by one-half to two-thirds from the top. At that point, most of the nutritional content within the foliage has transferred to the bulb, so you can snip the leaves off at ground level.

Like a fine wine with cheese, a perfect match is found in this pairing of pale-pink tulips with a soft-white hyacinth.

We now know to leave the leaves, but that could also make the garden look untidy, so here are a few tips for keeping those yellowing leaves relatively neat and orderly:

1. If you're planting in clumps (I recommend you use this planting method, see page 101) you can use string or a large elastic band to tie all the greens together into a tight bunch. This will contain the leaves so that they're not sprawling over a larger portion of the garden.

2. If you've planted bulbs individually, then you might want to consider tying all of the leaves of that single bulb into a loose knot.

3. Your final option is to dig up the bulbs—and please move on to our next question for more on this!

Q.

I have spring-blooming bulbs (tulips, daffodils and hyacinths) planted in pots. Is it okay to move the bulbs with their foliage so that I can plant something else in their place once they have finished flowering?

If you like the colour blue, then you must try growing this grape hyacinth (Muscari armeniacum). These beauties are hardy to zone 4, bloom abundantly, naturalize easily and provide good colour contrast.

A. Yes, you can pull them out, but leave the greens intact and rest them on their sides in a shaded part of the garden. This allows the foliage to die back naturally and the nutrition to transfer back into the bulbs. Position them slightly upright and leaning against one another, with just enough soil over the bulbs so that they're not showing.

In early summer, once the leaves have yellowed by one-half to two-thirds from the top—this should take a good month—remove the foliage with a sharp knife or pruners.

It's fine to leave the bulbs in this storage or resting area all summer and then replant them in fall in your pots or garden in anticipation of the following spring. (Maybe make a note on your calendar to plant them come October, because they're "heeled in" and outta sight and, well, outta mind.)

Another option is that once the leaves have died back, you can simply cut the leaves off at bulb level and store the bulbs in a paper bag or cardboard box in a cool location (below 65F/18C) until you're ready to plant them again in the fall.

Left: *An up-close look at hyacinth 'Anne Marie'. The fragrance of all hyacinths is amazing and can fill a room when forced for indoors or brought in as a cut flower.*
Below: *Drifts of yellow daffodils flow through this field. NFBIC photo*

A window box planter brimming with spring colour. Composed of tulips, mini daffodils, primrose, ivy and purple pansies, this look is easy to achieve. All the components can be purchased separately and arranged in pots or planters to grace your porches, windows and entryways.

DIVIDING PERENNIALS

How and when should I divide my hosta?

Dividing a hosta, or any other perennial for that matter, is basically a process of splitting the mother plant into two to four parts that will become independent new plants.

For someone cheap like me, it's a perfect means to expand my landscape at no cost. It's not always the best design idea, though, as you can easily identify a yard where the owner has learned the process of dividing perennials. In my opinion, there should never be more than two or three of the same plant within a yard. There are many obvious exceptions of course, including hedging material, groundcovers or plants of the same family but differing variety, such as the rhododendron or hydrangea, and, of course, food crops.

Sticking that fork through the heart of a hosta's root structure is daunting for most people. No one wants to make a mistake as to where to split the perennial.

But relax. It's actually a relatively easy process and in some cases imperative for ensuring the long-term health of the plant, rejuvenating it with what is

Hostas make a great border for shade or part-sun beds. There is much variety in leaf colours, from solid greens or blues to bicolour leaves with white or lime centres and margins.

essentially a form of root pruning. To lessen your jitters, it helps to know that it's nearly impossible to make a mistake.

The best method of dividing your hosta is to completely dig it out. As the root system is quite dense and compact, getting it out of the ground should be easy if you simply work your spade as deeply as possible around the entire plant just beyond the root zone. Be careful to find that sweet spot where the spade easily penetrates the earth without slicing into any roots. Next, you might have to slide the spade underneath the clump to pry it out of the ground as the final step in unearthing.

Once the hosta is out of the hole, you will require two garden forks. You can chop the clump into four even sections with a shovel, but my preference is to insert two forks, back to back, into the centre of the clump and pry the plant apart. This separates the clump in a more natural fashion.

Far left: Hostas, hardy from zones 3 to 9, are a staple in western gardens.
Left: The fat-ribbed leaf of this hosta adds form to your garden, and the solid-green colour adds contrast to surrounding blooms.

Once the clump is in two sections, divide them into two more. I don't usually recommend splitting the mother clump into more than four pieces.

The best time to consider splitting perennials is mid March to April, after all fear of heavy frost is gone. February is also acceptable in more temperate regions.

So if you end up with four or more hostas ready for planting, consider placing them in pots and giving them away as birthday presents, charity or plant-sale donations, hostess gifts or to neighbours so that you don't destroy the look of your yard with too much of a good thing.

SLUG IT OUT

Slugs and snails love hosta, so here's how to keep them at bay. Make up a simple solution of one part chlorine bleach to nine parts water. Using a watering can or bucket, drench emerging hosta shoots in spring to kill overwintering eggs and any young slugs or snails.

There are a number of different slug varieties, and they all like to dine in our yards. Control them early in the season at the first sign of nibble damage.

Q. We just moved into a new home with many tall bearded iris plants that have long since overgrown themselves. Can I divide these without digging the entire plant out of the ground (so that I can keep them where they are and ensure they still bloom this spring)?

Left: *A colourful bearded iris (Iris germanica 'Batik') rises above a grouping of white flowering candytuft.*
Right: *Bearded iris, zones 4 to 10, grow all over the world and require little or no care once established.*

A. Like most perennials, bearded irises can become very overgrown, often to a point where they're no longer attractive.

It's also true that bearded iris, like most perennials, should be divided on average every three years to rejuvenate and encourage the plant to perform more like its youthful former self. It's kind of like sending it to the spa.

Dividing plants can be intimidating, but it's really very easy and the chance of doing irreparable damage is virtually nil if you do it at the right time of year. Late winter/early spring is the ultimate time to divide perennials.

I usually suggest that you break a perennial clump into four pieces; however, an iris cluster can grow to more than 6 ft. (1.8 m) in diameter if it's not divided, and with its bulbous root structure, you can separate it into dozens of pieces simply by pulling the cluster apart by hand, depending on its size.

Replant four to six of those divisions in the same location you took them from, thoroughly mixing 22 lb. (10 kg) of fresh earth and 2 cups (500 mL) of bone meal into the planting area. You really should lift the entire patch and thin and divide, as by the sounds of it, this might never have been done. This won't affect your blooming and in fact might enhance it for the coming year, as the division will energize the plant.

DESIGN WISE…

>   Resist the urge to plant the remaining divisions anywhere and everywhere throughout your garden. A classy and tidy landscape is made up of a wide assortment of trees, shrubs and flowers, with attributes that complement each other and offer varying highlights at different times of the year (for more on this, see page 93).

The hardy lupine (Lupinus), zone 3, self-seeds readily and can be seen growing in meadows, ravines and roadside ditches across BC.

LOVELY LUPINES

My neighbour has a patch of lupines and I'm quite taken with them, as they self-seed and bloom on and on through the summer—what can you tell me about them?

Q.

A. Lupines are one of the most dramatic perennials in the garden and available in many pastel shades of blue, lavender, pink, red, white, yellow and bicolour. The pea-like flowers form along spikes that reach 2–3 ft. (60–90 cm), and the flat, palmate, or fan-shaped, leaves are also very attractive. You'll often see native lupines in bloom from May until August on hillsides throughout British Columbia, as they reseed themselves abundantly and are hardy to zone 3.

The more commonly grown Russell lupines are shorter and more compact than the wild version and fit easily into any garden setting. To grow lupines successfully, never fertilize them and don't disturb the roots when weeding around them. They prefer free-draining soil and full sun to part shade. They are susceptible to powdery mildew if grown in too shady a location. Dead-heading will encourage additional flower spikes later in the season, but if you want your plants to reseed, leave a few spent flower spikes on the plant. Slugs, snails and aphids are attracted to lupines, so control these pests as they arise (see pages 220 and 217).

DEALING WITH DEER

Q. *The deer are eating everything in my garden—is there anything I can plant that will still be there in the morning?*

A. Oh dear…I've spoken to many people so frustrated by the damage to and destruction of their plants by deer that they're ready to buck-shot Bambi. But they're so darn cute! The deer, that is—not necessarily the fuming gardeners.

Deer are part of the landscape in many communities, and although there is some truth in the observation that if they are hungry enough they will eat pretty much anything, there are plants deer generally shy away from. We'll define these flowers and shrubs as "deer resistant" and not "deer *proof*," just to be safe.

Here are some of my favourites, chosen for ease of care, good colour and ongoing interest:

Deer-resistant Plants

The zones indicated in this book are the minimum hardiness zones per genus. Individual cultivar hardiness zones could vary. Check with your local nursery for clarification.

SHRUBS AND TREES

- **Barberry (*Berberis*)** – zone 5, many varieties with different coloured foliage and mature heights, thorns
- **Beautybush (*Kolkwitzia amabilis*)** – zone 5, soft-pink, bell-shaped flowers in late spring
- **Dwarf purple rhododendron (*Rhododendron impeditum*)** – zone 5, slow growing to 1 ft. (30 cm), lilac-purple spring blooms
- **Japanese holly (*Ilex crenata*)** – zone 5, small glossy leaf, great for foundation planting
- **Kousa dogwood (*Cornus kousa*)** – zone 5, grows to 25 ft. (7.5 m), large white flowers in spring
- **Leyland cypress (× *Cupressocyparis leylandii*)** – zone 5, hedging tree, can grow up to 3 ft. (90 cm) per year
- **Mugo pine (*Pinus mugo*)** – zone 2, extremely hardy and adaptable conifer

- **Oregon grape (*Mahonia nervosa*)** – zone 6, slow-growing shrub with leaves that resemble holly, yellow flowers
- **Smokebush (*Cotinus coggygria*)** – zone 4, deep-maroon or bright-green round leaves, bush or tree form
- **Vine maple (*Acer circinatum*)** – zone 6, a native maple that likes wet sites

PERENNIALS AND BULBS

- **Alyssum (*Alyssum saxatilis*)** – zone 3, tough rockery perennial for sunny spots, covered in yellow flowers early spring
- **Autumn crocus (*Colchicum autumnale*)** – zone 5, fall-blooming crocus
- **Black-eyed Susan (*Rudbeckia*)** – zone 3, yellow and gold daisy-like flowers late summer through fall
- **Bleeding heart (*Dicentra spectabilis*)** – zone 3, heart-shaped, pink flowers on arching stems in early spring
- **Christmas rose (*Helleborus*)** – zone 4, blooms white or varying shades of pink mid winter, evergreen
- **Columbine (*Aquilegia*)** – zone 4, grows 1–4 ft. (30–120 cm), numerous colours of spring blooms
- **Daffodils (*Narcissus*)** – zone 3, large number of varieties of this early-spring-blooming bulb
- **Forget-me-not (*Myosotis sylvatica*)** – zone 5, early-spring clusters of bright-blue flowers
- **Heather (*Erica carnea*)** – zone 5, various shades of pink or white blooms, evergreen, border suitable
- **Lavender (*Lavandula augustifolia*)** – zone 5, heat and drought tolerant evergreen, fragrant purple bloom spikes

Left: Columbine (Aquilegia) *is an early-spring bloomer and a favourite of hummingbirds and bees. It is important to include plants that attract pollinating bees to your garden.*
Below: *Deer dislike plants with silver or grey foliage, such as lavender.*

Rhubarb leaves are poisonous, and deer instinctively avoid them.

- **Lily of the valley (*Convallaria*)** – zone 3, fragrant white bloom stems on 6-in. (15-cm) plants, groundcover, spreads rapidly
- **Ornamental onion (*Allium*)** – zone 3, many varieties, white or purple round blooms, taller types have very large flowers
- **Ostrich fern (*Matteuccia struthiopteris*)** – zone 3, grows to 4 ft. (120 cm), spreads by underground runners
- **Pigsqueak (*Bergenia*)** – zone 5, pink blooms above leathery evergreen foliage
- **Rhubarb (*Rheum*)** – zone 2, easy to grow, large leaves with edible red stalks
- **Rock cress (*Arabis*)** – zone 4, early-spring white blooms cover this low, mounding perennial
- **Rosemary (*Rosmarinus*)** – zone 5, evergreen-scented foliage, dislikes soggy sites, heat and drought tolerant
- **Sage (*Salvia officinalis*)** – zone 4, leaves can be green, purple or variegated, grows to 2 ft. (60 cm), use for culinary purposes
- **Shasta daisy (*Leucanthemum* × *superbum* 'Snowcap')** – zone 4, large, white daisy-like flowers from May to August
- **Siberian squill (*Scillia siberica*)** – zone 3, showy blue flowers in April, naturalizes
- **Thyme (*Thymus*)** – zone 5, there are 18 groundcover thymes and at least 10 culinary thymes, fragrant foliage when bruised, wee pink or purple blooms
- **Tickseed (*Coreopsis*)** – zone 4, summer blooming, many varieties, most grow to 2 ft. (60 cm)
- **Yarrow (*Achillea millefolium*)** – zone 3, multicoloured blooms on this hardy perennial for sunny, dry spots

Yarrow (Achillea) is a hardy perennial that blooms all summer and looks great in cut flower arrangements. It has silvery foliage.

Shrubs & Trees

Trees and shrubs are the main players of the garden. Although supporting characters may change from season to season, trees and shrubs remain the focus year in and year out.

As a key part of your landscape for what could be decades, trees and shrubs require some maintenance to keep them looking their best—otherwise, drastic measures might be called for to get your landscape looking picture perfect again.

And remember that even if you do things right, landscapes evolve over time and have a lifespan. Any yard will need either a partial or full overhaul after 15 years. Removing or moving some of the shrubs might be necessary, as plants often outgrow and crowd others; become aged to the point of being unattractive; or encroach on walkways, windows or doors.

Just knowing some basic tips for maintaining trees and shrubs, plus understanding a bit about the why and when-to for particular tasks, can go a long way to minimizing landscape overhauls and lessening tree and shrub loss.

A CLEAR VIEW

Choose plants wisely. Don't plant any shrub where it could cover or block any of your windows once it reaches its mature height.

ACIDIC SOIL

Q.

Thanks to a neighbour's large overhanging cedar tree, our soil is acidic—what shrubs or plants will survive in acidic soil?

A.

Cedars acidify the soil they grow in, creating an environment in which they thrive but many other trees, shrubs and perennials do not.

Nutrients become locked up and unavailable to plants when the soil is too acidic, starving plants. Many plants simply cannot tolerate an acidic soil and will decline if steps are not taken to counteract the acidity.

The one growth that you could potentially have an abundance of is moss. If you don't want moss, or would like to prevent it, you can add copious amounts of lime two or three times a year to raise the pH of the soil. This will also improve the growing conditions for many plants, as well as your lawn, and shouldn't harm the nearby cedar.

You may, however, simply want to consider choices that are tolerant of a low-pH soil. Here are my favourite acid-loving plants:

Originating in Missouri, this new false cypress (Chamaecyparis pisifera 'Soft Serve') is suited to small gardens, as it grows only 6–10 ft. (1.8–3 m). Hardy to zone 5, it is a graceful addition to urban outdoor spaces. Proven Winners photo

Previous page: *Regular maintenance keeps all growth (evergreen and deciduous) in check, preserving the original garden design.*

Acid Lovers

Rock daphne (Daphne cneorum) is known for being temperamental, but the fragrant blooms make up for it.

The zones indicated in this book are the minimum hardiness zones per genus. Individual cultivar hardiness zones could vary. Check with your local nursery for clarification.

- **Azaleas and rhododendrons (*Rhododendron*)** – zone 5, multicoloured early- and mid-spring bloomers, evergreen, low maintenance
- **Bog rosemary (*Andromeda polifolia*)** – zone 3, evergreen, low and mounding, delicate pink, bell-shaped flowers in spring
- **Bugleweed (*Ajuga reptans*)** – zone 3, hardy groundcover with dark foliage, purple spiked flowers
- **Camellia (*Camellia japonica*)** – zone 7, multicoloured, glossy leaves, evergreen
- **False spirea (*Astilbe*)** – zone 3, feathery plumes of red, pink or white in spring, herbaceous perennial

Left: *This evergreen azalea 'Rosebud' blooms for six weeks with perfectly rosebud-shaped flowers. A slow grower, this shrub will not quickly overpower its neighbours.*

Right: *Bog rosemary (Andromeda polifolia) is a low-growing flowering evergreen that prefers moist, acidic soil. Its blue foliage looks like the herb rosemary but is not edible. Bubblegum-pink blooms appear in spring.*

- **Heather (*Erica carnea*)** – zone 4, mounding evergreen, multicoloured, can be either spring, summer or winter blooming
- **Lily-of-the-valley shrub (*Pieris japonica*)** – zone 6, spring blooms of white or pink, evergreen, colourful new growth
- **Mountain laurel (*Kalmia latifolia*)** – zone 6, pink or red June flowers, evergreen, shade loving
- **Pigsqueak (*Bergenia*)** – zone 5, pink blooms above leathery evergreen foliage
- **Skimmia (*Skimmia japonica*)** – zone 7, deep-green broadleaf evergreen, red berries, shade tolerant

Top: Camellia 'Greensboro Red' produces semi-double flowers in a faded red. At maturity, it can reach up to 12 ft. (3.6 m) tall, with deep-green, glossy leaves.
Bottom: If you need a hardy, low-maintenance shrub for a low hedge, this skimmia variety (Skimmia japonica 'Rubella') is a solid choice.

This slow-growing lily of the valley (Pieris japonica 'Variegata') has colourful evergreen foliage and clusters of bell-shaped, white blooms in spring.

MULCH MIXES

Several years ago you gave out a recipe for shrub mulch mix on the radio. I used it every year with great success but have now lost it. Please repeat it!

Q.

A. Mulching—adding a mixed medium around the base of the plant—is an amazing way to assist your garden in becoming the best it can be.

Every year, spread mulch in a 2-in. (5-cm) layer over the root system of your plants and trees, out to the drip line. (But leave 1 ft./30 cm between mulch and tree trunks, as placing mulch too close can create a habitat for rodents that chew bark and girdle trees.)

There are many benefits of mulching:

- Mulch can insulate roots during cold winter spells.
- Mulch will protect the plant from drying out in the summer. Drying out puts stress on the plant, preventing it from performing as it should and making it more vulnerable to insects and disease.
- Plants can also root upwards into the mulch, thereby creating a larger root system that in turn will strengthen the plant in many ways.

I like to recommend the following mulch topping to be placed around the base of plants once a year, usually in spring. Mix together thoroughly:

(1 cu. ft.) 28 L mushroom manure
(1 cu. ft.) 28 L peat moss or coir
(1.5 cu. ft.) 40 L topsoil or compost
2 cups (500 mL) slow-release lawn fertilizer containing iron

Did you know a honey bee has such a well-defined sense of smell, it can differentiate hundreds of different floral varieties from across your yard?

Q. *Could you kindly reprint your recipe for a mulch to use around rhodos—mine need some perking up!*

A. Your rhododendrons will definitely benefit from this nourishing mulch—apply it every spring for good results:

22 lb. (10 kg) mushroom manure
22 lb. (10 kg) bark mulch
1 cup (250 mL) rhododendron fertilizer
4 Tbsp (60 mL) micronized iron, chelated iron or fritted trace elements

Mix together thoroughly and spread in a 2-in. (5-cm) layer from the trunk to the drip line of each rhodo.

A grouping of well-established rhododendrons in a woodland setting. Rhododendrons can live for up to 100 years, or even longer.

INTERNET CAUTION

I read on the Internet that my newly purchased evergreen magnolia will grow 100 ft. (30 m). Will it grow that big in my small yard in southwestern British Columbia?

Q.

A. You really need to be careful with information you get off the Internet about plants.

Yes, a *Magnolia grandiflora* can grow to more than 100 feet…in California! But a *Magnolia grandiflora* grown around the forty-ninth parallel won't get anywhere near that height, for a variety of reasons mostly related to the climate. In cool but temperate climates, the *Magnolia grandiflora* will only reach a height of approximately 40 ft. (12 m), and that is without any pruning. *Magnolia grandiflora* can tolerate zones 6–10, so it has limitations and will not grow in many parts of North America.

From region to region, soil conditions, climate and the preferred varieties vary:

Lawn maintenance and grass choices differ from place to place. In

This saucer magnolia (Magnolia x soulangiana), zone 4, is a small, low-branched tree that flowers before it leafs out in the early spring.

Magnolias are available in a wide assortment of varieties with varying shapes, sizes and colours of blooms. Choose one that best suits your area.

California, for example, a heat-tolerant grass is necessary and is a completely different lawn than what you would see in Metro Vancouver, which is different from northern British Columbia, which is different from the Prairies.

Instructions for growing a bougainvillea over an arbour in your yard are not appropriate for northern gardeners, as it is not a hardy plant and won't survive cold winters.

The care and maintenance of your rose bush is completely different in Calgary than in Vancouver.

Peaches grow extremely well in dry and hot summer climates but are a challenge in moist coastal regions.

I think you get the idea, and I could go on and on to make the point that it is imperative you ensure the information you are referencing is written for your region.

You've made a wise choice in purchasing this book, and, by the way, thanks. My prediction is that this whole Internet thing is just a phase. The typewriter will be back before you know it.

REBELLIOUS ROSES

Q. *My 'Oregold' rose failed to produce flowers last year—it grew very tall with healthy leaves but did not bloom, whereas the rest of my roses did. What went wrong?*

A. Although it is hard to say specifically why the rose didn't bloom, no matter what variety we are talking about, the problem is most often the result of one or more of the following four situations:

1. Insufficient pruning in spring. All hybrid tea, grandiflora and floribunda roses should be pruned relatively hard by March. Usually a more moderate pruning is completed in the fall, followed by this final hard pruning done in March. Generally speaking, from the ground up, these should be the final heights: hybrid tea roses 12–18 in. (30–45 cm) and floribunda and grandiflora 18–24 in. (45–60 cm). (For more on this, see page 204.)

2. Too much shade. If rose bushes don't get enough sun, they will not set a flower bud.

3. Too much manure or nitrogen-rich fertilizer. This is the least likely scenario, as even if there was too much nitrogen, you would still most likely get some blooms. Nevertheless, use one of the many rose-specific soluble fertilizers available from your local garden centre and feed your rose bushes every two weeks from May through September.

4. The final and more common possibility is that the rose may have died from the graft up over winter. Often gardeners see that the rose is growing and assume that it's the top graft, but it's actually the understock. See the next question for more on this.

The largest rose blooms can be found in the group called hybrid teas. They are grown commercially for the cut flower market and remain the most popular flowering shrub in our yards today.

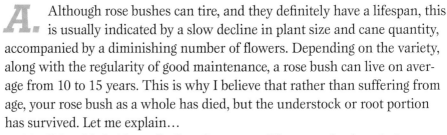

Q. I have two ten-year-old rose bushes that stopped blooming and just keep growing taller. Is it time to replace them?

A. Although rose bushes can tire, and they definitely have a lifespan, this is usually indicated by a slow decline in plant size and cane quantity, accompanied by a diminishing number of flowers. Depending on the variety, along with the regularity of good maintenance, a rose bush can live on average from 10 to 15 years. This is why I believe that rather than suffering from age, your rose bush as a whole has died, but the understock or root portion has survived. Let me explain…

Traditional hybrid tea, floribunda, or grandiflora rose-bush varieties are all a combination of two different plants. The rootstock is traditionally from a hardier family of rose, sometimes even a wild rose, onto which breeders graft a second variety, usually one with special attributes such as large flowers, unique colours or supreme fragrance. Breeders really never know what the end result might be, however. Mixing A + B does not always = C. Breeders are continually trying to come up with that perfect combination—the "Holy Grail of Roses"—with intense bloom colour and fragrance, along with durability, disease resistance and cold tolerance.

What happens periodically in the garden is that for some reason, usually winterkill, the upper rose variety dies. A prolonged cold spell can sometimes be too much for the unprotected upper portion of the rose. The understock, however—normally the hardier variety and also more protected from the elements, being that it's underground—survives. Without an outlet for this understock to dispense the energy that would normally go to the upper portion of the rose, it instead sends growth from its own root system, which becomes the new rose. Unfortunately, the understock is more of a wild variety and will not necessarily bloom for you. The leaves of this new rose also often differ from what you previously had, and you'll find the plant quite vigorous.

The answer? Pull it out. Well, that is unless you like the green bushy shrub that now sits where you once admired your colourful and fragrant rose.

Miniature roses can be used in flower beds and containers. Ensure good winter protection, as they are less hardy than full-sized roses.
Proven Winners photo

SUMMER-BLOOMING SHRUBS

I don't have a lot of space in my garden but would like a shrub or two that will offer good colour throughout the summer. What's the best choice?

Q.

A. That's a tough question! How do I pick just one or two from the dozens that I love? It's almost like trying to pick one of your children as a favourite. Every child and every plant has their moments both good and bad, and every plant has its particular attributes.

Take one of my favourites, for example: I love Bruns Serbian spruce (*Picea omorika* 'Bruns'). This is a slender spruce with a silvery undertone to its needles. It is very stately, with a West Coast flavour, and looks spectacular in the right spot. Without flowers and with limited colour, it makes a gorgeous statement, all the same.

From perennial to annual, shrub to tree, variety is endless, so the key is to select the right mix for your yard. I often mention how a garden centre is a wealth of knowledge and experience…and product. And as the centre tends to stock or highlight what is in bloom at the time, by visiting regularly, you can gradually ensure that your garden is filled with blooms and other attributes that take you right through the year.

Here is one of my biggest pieces of advice for filling your yard with year-round colour. Do not do all your shopping in one weekend! Often homeowners will decide to renovate or complete their landscape—or maybe they bought a new house and they're going to install a whole new yard—and they head down to their local garden centre and purchase pretty much everything that is in bloom. How can you blame them? It's hard to resist flowers and colour. The end result, however, is that they will have a yard filled with colour every year in that same month they purchased everything that was in bloom. The rest of the year…nada.

Piece together your landscape over time, with plants that will fill your yard with colour every single month of the year. Sometimes this may be the bright branches of a yellow twig dogwood or coral bark maple, other months the brilliant-orange leaves of a burning bush—but every month you'll be enjoying something amazing in your garden.

The following are some of the most popular summer-blooming shrubs, because of their fragrance, their colourful leaves or other attributes:

Summer-blooming Shrubs

The zones indicated in this book are the minimum hardiness zones per genus. Individual cultivar hardiness zones could vary. Check with your local nursery for clarification.

- **Abelia (*Abelia × grandiflora* AGM)** – zone 6, pale-pink, slightly fragrant summer blooms, arching branches
- **Blue mist shrub (*Caryopteris*)** – zone 6, green or variegated foliage, true blue-coloured blooms
- **Hydrangea (*Hydrangea*)** – zones 3 to 6, depending on variety, blooms summer through fall, multicoloured, masses of flowers
- **Littleleaf lilac (*Syringa pubescens* ssp. *microphylla* 'Superba')** – zone 5, scented, pinky-lavender blooms, heat and drought tolerant
- **Ninebark (*Physocarpus opulifolius*)** – zone 3, pink or white blooms, purple or yellow foliage
- **Rose of Sharon (*Hibiscus syriacus*)** – zone 6, multicoloured flowers all summer, in tree or bush form
- **Summersweet (*Clethra alnifolia*)** – zone 4, fragrant spiky, white flowers
- **Weigela (*Weigela florida* 'Minuet')** – zone 4, dwarf shrub with purplish red flowers on purple-tinged foliage

My 'Monet'™ weigela (Weigela florida 'Sunset'), zone 5, is valued for its multicoloured foliage and dwarf, compact size (growing 12–18 in./30–45 cm). Proven Winners photo
***Right**: Picture this hydrangea (Hydrangea paniculata 'Bobo'™), zone 5, impressing your neighbours and passersby with its masses of huge white blossoms. Proven Winners photo*

BEE SMART

When planting a shrub near or around your patio, ensure it is not a bee magnet, such as a California lilac, which will have insects buzzing around your outdoor seating or eating area. Place bee-attracting plants a little farther afield.

Left: *Korean lilacs offer incredible fragrance and grow to a height of only 4 ft. (120 cm).*

Below: *Developed in France, this double white lilac (Syringa vulgaris 'Madame Lemoine') has intensely fragrant blooms.*

LILAC PROBLEMS

My lilac won't bloom! It looks healthy, grows well and, other than a few spots on the leaves, is fine. What's wrong with it?

Q.

A. Since my father is known as the "Lilac King," because he grows tens of thousands of lilacs for resale across North America, I would have to say that lilacs are part of my blood. And I don't know about you, but I can't walk by a lilac and not have a little sniff.

There is nothing more frustrating than having a lilac in your yard that won't bloom. Okay…my kids leaving the fridge door open is up there too, but let's get back to your bloom-deprived plant.

There are three common reasons why a lilac won't bloom:

1. It must be located in a bright, full-on sunny location. If not…your lilac won't bloom. Moving the plant would be my one and only recommendation if you have it in a shaded location; otherwise, enjoy the green.

2. Lilacs are alkaline-loving plants. Too acidic a soil and…you guessed it—your lilac won't bloom. Using a pH test kit (available at garden centres), check the soil near the lilac to quickly give you an answer. Some regions of the country are traditionally alkaline or acidic. Metro Vancouver, for example, is an acidic-soil region, and if you're trying to grow a lilac in this area, don't even bother testing your soil—just add lime. For a chronically low-pH region, I usually recommend adding 10 lb. (4.5 kg) of dolomite lime per lilac plant twice a year, once in February and again in October. This should keep the soil pH at more than 7 on the pH scale, which is the lowest that it can be to ensure blooming success.

3. And, lastly, accurate timing of pruning ensures flowering the following year. It's very important to prune your lilac shortly after blooming. Pruning at any other time could potentially remove the flower buds for the following year…and your lilac won't bloom. (For more on pruning lilacs, see page 211.)

If you keep these three pointers in mind, I smell the fragrance of lilacs in your future.

Left: Originally from Europe and Asia, lilacs have been growing in North America since at least 1750. Sunshine and alkaline soil will guarantee success with the lilac family.
Right: *White is not the most popular colour for lilacs; however, their fragrance and beauty stand out in a vase.*

HAPPY HEDGES

I need a tall, narrow, fast-growing evergreen hedge to cover a large unsightly fence our neighbours just erected.

Q.

A. Depending on the height that you'd like this hedge to grow, one of your best options is a western red cedar.

I had a similar situation in my yard and needed a narrow, tall screen fast.

I planted western red cedars, and they quickly offered me a screen. To keep them narrow, though, there needs to be some commitment to trimming: initially, I was shearing them a couple of times a year but was able to reduce it to once a year as they aged. Make sure you do a complete shearing of the sides once a year in spring or fall. Without routine maintenance, the western red cedar can become a giant. I've managed to keep the hedge to a 4-ft (120-cm) width, and believe it or not, they now stand more than 30 ft. (9 m) tall. Yup, I got my screen! I could have topped them to keep them much shorter, but that height gave me what I wanted.

Western reds are native to British Columbia, so they enjoy a more "liquid" climate. They are also very pest resistant. Cedars are a popular hedge of choice across Canada and the northern United States, and there are quite a number of varieties available. However, some varieties have temperature limitations, so you would be wise to choose one that is cold hardy enough for your particular climate.

This well-maintained cedar hedge (Thuja occidentalis 'Smaragd'), zones 2–7, provides privacy and a sound buffer, looks much nicer than a fence and is more economical long term.

A type of cedar that is far more popular than the western red is the *Thuja occidentalis* 'Smaragd' (zones 2–7). This is the most popular cedar in many parts of North America, because it only grows to a maximum of 2 ft. (60 cm) wide by about 12 ft. (3.6 m) tall.

Hedging plays an important part in so many of our yards as a visual screen and sound buffer. Choose wisely and maintain regularly for a beautiful and more ecological long-term alternative to a high-maintenance fence.

Q. *The deer enjoy munching on the bottom branches of my 13-ft. (4-m) cedar hedge. If I trimmed it to half its height, would it survive and might this encourage the bottom to rejuvenate?*

A. Deer do enjoy a meal of cedar hedge, with the end result being a thin base as high as they are able to reach to feed and then a flaring out to normal width to the top of the hedge. It definitely does not make for an attractive hedge—instead it tends to look a bit like a row of green popsicles.

If you want to grow cedar hedges in an area where deer like to dine, I suggest that you trim the hedge biannually to ensure each tree is cropped tight.

Give your established hedges some general maintenance yearly and they will reward you by always looking good.

You'll do this for two reasons. First, it's a little more difficult for the deer to feast on a regularly sheared hedge. Second, by keeping the hedge trimmed narrow, the eaten portion of the tree will be less visible than on a hedge allowed to grow to its full width up top. You simply trim the upper portion of the tree to match the width of the lower deer-nibbled section.

Alternatively, you can wrap chicken wire around each tree to a height of 5 ft. (1.5 m) and keep the tree trimmed to just outside the chicken wire (or allow the deer to eat it to the wire). Obviously, you'd have to keep the upper portion trimmed to that width as well. The benefit of this option, however, is that you can wrap the chicken wire to a greater width so that the deer can't sheer the tree to spindle width.

An amazingly effective organic repellent is called Plantskydd. When it is applied monthly to the base of the cedar, or any plant, deer avoid it.

And to answer your questions, cedar is very resilient and can tolerate being trimmed by up to half. A little grooming and tapering at the top will be necessary, and if you cut them too low, the barren centres may be visible and will not grow back. All the remaining exterior of the tree, however, should look fine.

Just because you've trimmed the tree down does not mean that the deer won't continue to feed on it, nor will cutting the trees down encourage additional bottom growth. Since you're considering an overhaul to the hedge, you might actually want to think about changing out the cedars for a deer-proof option. Japanese cedar (*Cryptomeria japonica*) and Japanese yew (*Taxus cuspidata*) are two great options for a deer-resistant hedge.

Q.

How can I prevent the inside of my junipers and cedar hedge from going brown?

A. It's not only junipers and hedging cedars that are going to have dead needles at their centre. Any plant that grows dense enough to eliminate light within is going to develop brown leaves or needles because of corresponding lack of light. Leaves and needles both require light to survive, and as the outer growth of a plant develops, it will start to shade the earlier growth.

Actually, this isn't a problem for your plants but rather a way of securing the spot in which they are growing. Plants can and do create their own mulch by shedding interior needles and leaves that can fall, rot and become humus. The plant then has added material to grow roots into, making it stronger and more able to compete. A plant's own needles or leaves are the best possible mulch, as they contain all the elements that particular plant needs as a continual base to grow and expand.

Interior browning is increased even more when junipers and hedges are sheared and pruned, as this increases the density of their foliage, further shading the interior of the plants.

Again, the browning of the interior growth is normal behaviour for plants, so there's not necessarily a requirement to take any action. In a natural setting, this debris would benefit the plants, but in our yards with our regular watering and feeding, its removal helps to keep the yard tidy and free of clutter.

It is advisable, therefore, to annually clean out some of the dead leaves and needles that might not have fallen to the ground. Often they become stuck on branches and build up into a clump, harbouring insects and disease. The best way to eliminate the debris inside your plants is with a pressure nozzle on a hose. Simply spray through the hedge or shrub and pressure-wash the debris out.

Removing the debris annually is good maintenance, kind of like changing the oil in a car. A little upkeep can prevent a lot of problems in the future.

Q. *We had to severely prune back a shrub between two very tall columnar cedars, and now there are large bare spots showing on the cedars where they were pressed against it. Will this grow back now?*

A. Yours is not an uncommon problem. Cedars can be burdened with bare spots for a number of reasons. No matter how or where the bare spots are on your cedar, there are actions that you can take to repair and improve the aesthetics of the plant.

First, keep hedging cedars trimmed regularly. The sides as well as the top need at least an annual shearing. This will keep the trees relatively rigid and prevent some of the problems that can be caused by snowload during the winter months. A secondary shearing in late summer is very beneficial as a means to keep them dense and neat.

Opposite: Do not allow shrubs to crowd your hedge. Shear shrubs regularly to maintain air flow and light penetration between them and the hedge.

Also, ensure that no other plant material grows up to and against your hedging cedars, as a lack of light or a complete sheltering will kill those areas of the hedge. Often the hedge is located at the back of a garden that is brimming with other plant material. Keep in mind that plants in front of the hedge need to be trimmed as they grow so that they don't rub against it. Add new plants strategically, keeping in mind their growth habits, height and width to ensure they are positioned far enough away from the hedge to avoid contact. Any part of the hedging that has had limited light for a period of six months or longer will start to suffer and decline.

Regenerating growth from needle-less mature stems within the tree is unlikely. The only option for filling barren spots within the hedge is some reconstructive surgery or reconfiguration of the branching. Using Soft-Tie or Vinyl-Tie, or a similar pliable stretch material, you can move branches by redirecting and securing them to other branches within the tree. Soft-Tie or Vinyl-Tie is strong enough to hold the branches yet pliable enough not to girdle or strangle them as they grow. I have pulled and secured branches quite aggressively, with an end result of a complete repair and filling-in of the bare spots.

Q. *Why do my hedging cedars have little bits of yellowing here and there toward the end of summer?*

A. Toward the end of summer, many cedar varieties show small amounts of yellowing of their leaves (needles) throughout the tree. This is not uncommon and is actually quite normal and labelled as "flagging."

Although it is not a result of an insect or disease, and is generally part of

an inherent thinning process, flagging can also be a sign of a lack of water throughout a hot summer. A thorough, deep watering with a sprinkler for two hours every two weeks through hot spells should help to prevent your cedar trees from flagging.

Q. *We will be moving in February and are unable to take our large and lovely ruby weigela with us. Can we take cuttings and try to plant them?*

A. The good news is that weigela is quite easy to propagate. This is usually done by taking cuttings early in the season (June) just prior to blooming and can also be done later in the season following bloom (October/November). Here's how:

This red weigela, zone 4, is one of 180 cultivars. Tough, hardy and attractive, weigelas are perfect low-maintenance accent plants.

1. Take a 6-in. (15-cm) cutting at least 6 in. (15 cm) back from the end of a mature branch.

2. Make a clean cut right below a node (the part of the stem from which a leaf, branch or aerial root grows).

3. Remove any leaves on the bottom half of the cutting and dip that end in a rooting hormone. The rooting hormone is a very important step in the process, as it will help to stimulate the branch into producing the chemicals it needs to grow roots.

4. Now the cutting is ready to be inserted 2 in. (5 cm) into a container filled with a soil-less mix (commercial starter mix, or a combination of 50 percent sand and 50 percent pre-moistened coir or vermiculite). Do not let the soil go dry through the rooting process.

5. Enclose the entire pot or tray of cuttings in a dry-cleaner bag or other large, clear plastic bag and place it outside but out of direct sun.

6. Now it's time to be the patient gardener. It will take approximately one month for the stems to show signs of rooting from a June cutting and up to two months from the late-fall cutting. Tug gently on the cutting after that period, and if you feel resistance, the cutting has rooted and could be potted up or planted out anytime thereafter.

And if I could have the last word? Just because you can take cuttings from a plant doesn't always mean that you should. If a variety of plant is easy to propagate, it will probably be a common plant. Over this past decade, plant breeders have developed hundreds of new plant species that perform better, are hardier, more fragrant, more compact, more disease resistant, more productive, and so on. So you may not want to fill the valuable space in your garden with the same-old, when you might be much happier with the new-improved.

Propagating other trees…

Most deciduous shrubs are propagated similarly to the weigela; however, the timing is usually different. The rule of thumb is to propagate in late winter, prior to them setting out leaf or flower, or after blooming but prior to the heat of summer.

A pink weigela (Weigela florida) will grow quickly and reach 6–9 ft. (1.8–2.7 m). Hummingbirds love this plant.

TREE CONCERNS

My street tree starts dropping leaves mid summer. Why is this and how can I stop it from happening?

Q.

A. For a number of reasons, it's not good that your street tree is dropping leaves.

First, it makes a mess—but you already know that.

Second, the tree is showing you that it is under stress, which is unhealthy for the tree and makes it more susceptible to insects and diseases.

And third, that tree is not working at its full potential to cleaning the air that we breathe.

For the most part, there are two reasons a street tree will drop its leaves mid summer:

Lack of water through summer

The most common reason that a street tree will drop its leaves prematurely is a lack of water. But even if you watered it regularly, this might not be enough.

Watering a street tree is different from irrigating any other plant in your yard. The tree's roots are possibly growing under hot pavement and cement sidewalks, both of which retain heat and block water from being absorbed into the ground and becoming available to the roots of the tree. Often, you'll see a little cut-out around a street tree, and many people think that this is the place to water. Not so much.

A shade tree doesn't have a lot of roots right around its trunk, so watering in that cute little cut-out is not going to quench its thirst. The roots can span many metres; therefore, a deep watering of any lawn or soil up to roughly 30 ft. (9 m) from the trunk will greatly assist the tree in acquiring moisture. One thorough, deep watering of the area for an hour or so a week should provide it with enough water so that it doesn't drop leaves in mid summer, assuming that a lack of moisture is the issue.

Compost leaves collected from your lawn, as they should not sit on the grass over winter. Fallen leaves can remain in flower beds, as they are nature's blanket, protecting plants' roots from freezing.

If your tree has struggled through a drought period, it is important to know that recovery will take some time, even if you start watering immediately. If the tree became excessively dry, leaves will continue to drop, because many of those leaves will have suffered internal damage beyond repair. The extent of cell damage to each leaf will determine its chances of recovery. So even with regular watering after a drought, your tree still could have a period of a month where affected leaves continue to drop.

This should show the importance of regular deep watering throughout its growing period and, more particularly, as the weather through summer starts to warm. Another gardener's tip is to jab your garden fork through the surface of the lawn or soil in and around the drip line of the tree once a month or so, from June through August, to allow water to better soak into the soil (as opposed to just running down the street into a culvert). Insert that garden fork at least 6 in. (15 cm) deep into the soil dozens of times all around the tree's absorption zone; this will also benefit any surrounding garden and lawn.

Infestation

Insect infestations or fungal or bacterial diseases can also damage the health of the leaves on your street tree. An aphid that sucks moisture and nutrition out of the leaves will slowly deteriorate the leaf until it is compromised to the point of no return…or, better put, to the point of return to the earth.

It's good to take a regular close look at your shrubs and trees—a plant may appear uninhabited from afar, but a more up-close and personal inspection may reveal it to be infested. If that's the case, have the foliage diagnosed by your local garden-centre expert so that you are able to control the problem before serious damage is done.

Q.

What can you suggest for a privacy tree for our backyard on the east side of the house? The tree will not receive morning sun but will get early-afternoon to evening sun through the summer. The tree needs to reach at least 30 ft. (9 m) at maturity.

A. Interestingly enough, I needed a similar tree for screening in my yard. Although there are a number of trees that could do the job, my number-one choice was *Styrax japonicus*, otherwise known as the Japanese snowbell tree. Its height is perfect, but any tree you decide on will take a little bit of annual maintenance to ensure success. The big issue is width—most shade trees have a tendency to offer breadth as well as height, and although the Japanese snowbell can grow to a moderate width, it is also a tree that can be kept relatively narrow.

Every year or two, following the show of a multitude of white (or pink) hanging bell-shaped flowers in June, I take a hedge trimmer to my Japanese snowbell and shear the sides to keep it narrow. As the tree has grown taller each year, I've also removed lower branches to keep the foliage above the fenceline, thereby eliminating any walk-by interference from branches. it's gorgeous and also very easy to grow, as it doesn't attract insects and is not partial to any particular soil composition. Lastly, it gets a nice bright-yellow fall colour! Is it the perfect tree for you?

Floral designers prize the deep-green, glossy leaf of the evergreen magnolia. The huge creamy-white summer blooms are stunning.

Of course, the downside is that it is deciduous and, therefore, would offer limited privacy or screening through the winter months. Nevertheless, it does have quite a healthy inner branching network, providing somewhat of a screen, probably enough for visual obstruction. The benefit of a deciduous tree is that it will allow more light indoors during darker months.

If you're looking for an evergreen, however, then I recommend the western red cedar (*Thuja plicata*). It, too, can grow wide and, therefore, would also require annual shearing to keep it narrow.

And there are two more trees that I'd also like you to consider.

Another evergreen option is the columnar broadleaf evergreen magnolia (*Magnolia grandiflora* columnar), which would tolerate your moderately sunny location and could also handle even more sun, if need be. It is stunning, with its glossy green leaves and fuzzy bronze undertone. You'll also enjoy its large white-cupped blossoms every summer. It does have cold limitations, however, and is limited to zone 6 and warmer.

An extremely cold-hardy and beautiful easy-to-grow columnar tree is the trembling aspen (*Populus tremuloides* columnar). The benefit of a columnar tree is that it offers height and is dense enough to offer privacy.

A neat row of well-maintained hedging provides a great windbreak, sound barrier and privacy screen. Not that we don't love our neighbours.

Containers &
Hanging Baskets

I f you are one of the many people today living in a condo or townhome, a container garden or windowbox might be the only part of your outdoor landscape you need to worry about. Or patio pots and colourful hanging baskets flanking your front door may be a big part of your home's outdoor décor.

THINK OUT OF
THE BASKET
A hanging basket
is simply a hanging
container…
so how about a
summer-blooming
groundcover rose
to brighten your
summer patio?

Either way, there is no denying the positive effect container gardening and hanging baskets can have on a home, small or large, with the possibilities being endless. Potted shrubs for structure, edibles, perennials and annuals can all make a strong statement and provide joy to the gardener.

By following some very simple steps and keeping in mind a few important tips, you can prevent your containers from going to pot (okay…bad pun) and take them from marginal to magical. Planters previously limited to summer display will become four-season showpieces, hanging baskets will flow with colour and texture, and you will enjoy them all to their maximum potential.

ANNUAL STRATEGY
Although I chop all of my annuals down in fall, I leave the root mass in the container to stabilize colourful twigs, cuttings of greens and stems with berries, which I poke into the soil for a festive look on my patio.

Q. *If I miss the spring planting season for my patio planters (as I often do because I am so busy!), is there a fast-growing solution for beautifying my patio for summer dinner parties?*

A. So, spring was busy for you and, before you know it, it's June and guests are coming over on the weekend. You want your patio looking bright and beautiful, but your planters are barren, and quickly planting up some small annuals for colour is just not going to cut it. Now what?

Well, I have just the solution.

Head down to your local garden centre and pick up three things: a lovely hanging basket, a large bag of planter-box soil, and a box of granular 6-8-6 fertilizer. Garden centres always have a great selection of lush and colourful hanging baskets in June, or anytime spring through mid summer, for that matter. What we're going to do is take that hanging basket and "drop" it into your container on your patio:

Instead of growing annuals in a hanging basket, try a groundcover rose. They can produce up to 2,000 blooms per season and don't require spraying, deadheading or fancy pruning.

1. First, remove any soil from your patio container to a depth of the height of the hanging-basket pot, and reuse that soil by placing it in and around plants in your garden. Then loosen the remaining soil in your patio container.

Scratch about 1 cup (250 mL) of the 6-8-6 fertilizer into that soil.

2. Now it's showtime. Remove the hangers from the hanging basket so that you're left with just the container, or replace all the soil with fresh planter box soil to a level that would allow the basket soil level to be flush with the top of the container.

3. Use the fingers of one hand to support the top of the planting by pressing against the soil (being careful not to bend or break any of the plants). Pick up the basket with the other hand and tip it over so that the upside-down basket of plants is balancing on your fingers.

4. Remove the pot from the hanging-basket rootball and gently turn the planting upright, and lower it into your patio container. Wow, it looks fantastic!

Dropping a hanging basket straight into a pot is a winning practice, because:
- *It's quick*
- *It's easy*
- *It's less expensive than purchasing each plant individually*
- *Plants are further ahead in their growth*
- *Combinations are already chosen for you by an expert*
- *It makes you look like a pro!*

5. Now you need to add some planter-box soil around the basket. This is easier with two people—one to hold up the leaves of the sprawling hanging plants, while the other pours the soil in and around the hanging-basket roots. You'll want to pack that soil down around the root system of the hanging basket by firmly pressing with your fingers all of the freshly added planter-box soil.

6. Now add 2 cups (500 mL) of 6-8-6 fertilizer around the entire basket on top of the fresh soil. Top up the soil again to just below the top of the container. Scratch an additional 1 cup (250 mL) of 6-8-6 around the top of the basket.

7. Thoroughly water the planter.

You've now created a masterpiece. Your guests will think that you're a brilliant gardener, and you and I will be the only two who have to know about this little trick of ours.

CONTAINER DRAINAGE

I understand that drainage is important in a container—how can I ensure that it is adequate in my outdoor pots? **Q.**

A. Good drainage in pots is not only important, it's vital. They go together like a hot dog and ketchup, or yam fries and ketchup, or a burger and ketchup. Guess what condiment I prefer for my patio barbecue meals?

But, seriously, success with growing in containers begins from the bottom up.

Without proper drainage, a pot can become a swimming pool rather than a vessel for growing in. Plants subjected to swampy soil because of poor drainage will begin to deteriorate almost instantly.

The roots of a plant must breath, so if they are submerged in water, the plant will drown. Initially, it will try to save itself by taking in as much of the water as it can, but it is only able to use so much—and the resulting combination of the roots being unable to breathe and the plant being waterlogged will cause it to wither away. Interestingly, at a certain saturation point, the roots become ineffective and can no longer draw water, so the plant actually starts to look like it is drying out prior to dying.

Any pot of less than 10 in. (25 cm) in diameter won't require too much additional effort when it comes to drainage, because it is small enough that you can manage the amount of water and easily check how much moisture is in the container with the old stick-the-finger-into-the-soil trick. Larger containers 12 in. (30 cm) in diameter or greater require adequate drainage holes for the size of the pot.

Start by ensuring that there are drain holes. Yes, I know that this might sound like a no-brainer, but often plastic containers, for example, come with what look like drain holes, but the tabs actually need to be punched out.

For containers 12 in. (30 cm) in diameter or greater, follow this chart for the optimum number and size of drainage holes:

Planting a single variety of this blue fescue (Festuca glauca) in a container is contemporary and bold.

Size of pot	Number of holes per pot	Size of hole
12 in. (30 cm) to 14 in. (35 cm)	3	1 in. (2.5 cm)
16 in. (40 cm) to 18 in. (45 cm)	3	1.5 in. (4 cm)
20 in. (50 cm) to 22 in. (55 cm)	4	1.5 in. (4 cm)
24 in. (60 cm) or greater	4	2 in. (5 cm)

If additional drainage is required, you can cut more holes through plastic with a regular drill bit or a sharp knife, drill holes through fibreglass or resin with a regular metal drill bit, or create additional holes in ceramic or clay-based pots with a masonry drill bit.

Next, fill your pots with a good-quality soil that is rich in organic matter. Adding perlite will also help to increase drainage throughout the soil.

Another problem is caused by placing flat-based pots against flat surfaces, impeding the outflow. If the water can't drain away out the bottom, it doesn't matter how many holes the pot has to start, or how many have been conscientiously drilled by you. Each container needs to be slightly elevated off the ground (about ½ to 1 in./1 to 2.5 cm) to enable water to efficiently drain out.

There are many pot-elevating options that you can buy—from pot pads made of a rubber component to pot feet of a more decorative nature. Or you can use just about anything. The dog's squeaky bone would do the trick; however, you would require three the very same size to elevate the pot evenly.

Finally, if you think the drain holes of any of your containers may be restricted, with the assistance of another person, tip the pot slightly so that you can access the bottom and push a stick or screwdriver into the drain holes, jiggling it around to clear them. This is a worthwhile spring task, assuming your pots are filled with perennial plants and not refilled each year with new annual plants and rejuvenated soil.

Choose unusual and non-traditional planting vessels to add interest to your arrangement, like this giant teacup!

LIGHTEN THINGS UP…

Pots too heavy to move around? Consider lightweight, durable fibreglass pots, with an inch or two of recycled Styrofoam packing chips at the bottom of the containers to reduce soil volume.

SOIL

What is the best soil for containers?

Q.

A. This is actually a tougher question than you might think, as there are so many soils on the market that it truly does get confusing.

For outdoor containers, I suggest you mix together two or more different soil blends. Diversity in the soil blend will be beneficial to the plants and, for example, mixing one soil with more of a loam base with another containing more of a compost base will make a more complex and rich soil.

I also suggest mixing roughly one bag of mushroom manure into your soil mix. Mushroom manure is a great soil additive, as it is very porous and abundant in the minerals and micro-nutrients container-grown plants may not otherwise have access to. A small investment in good-quality soil will make a tremendous difference to the success of your container garden. As you mix the mediums together thoroughly, add granular fertilizer for long-term feeding of the container plantings (see our next question for more on this).

You'll have noticed that I didn't go into great detail to recommend "one part of this to three parts of something else." This is simply not necessary… because your plants *want to grow*. In fact, they want to grow *so much* that they will tolerate poor or one-dimensional soil, given a little food and water. So if you simply heed my general advice about providing a mix of a couple of good soil blends, your plants are going to thrive.

Lastly, if you're in a garden centre looking for soil, don't ask for "dirt" or you just might get the hairy eyeball from the staff. "Dirt" is what you sweep off the floor, whereas "soil" is what makes your garden great!

With a keen eye for colour combinations, this freshly assembled planter began with adequate drainage and a good-quality potting mix.

HOW OFTEN DO WE NEED TO REPLACE THE SOIL IN OUR CONTAINER GARDENS?

People often ask me if the soil in containers needs to be replaced every year. They're referring to annual-flower container gardens, as opposed to perennial plants in containers. The answer is that although not *all* of the soil needs to be replaced, one-third to one-half should be exchanged with fresh soil and manure, which can be mixed thoroughly with what is left in the container.

Replacing some of the soil in your pots will reintroduce both nutrients and porous material that will loosen the overall soil composition, making it easier for the root system to penetrate. The faster and easier the root system can get established, the stronger and healthier the plant will be. Meanwhile, the old soil needn't be wasted—go ahead and add it to any outdoor landscaped areas.

FEEDING

 How often do I need to feed my container garden?

There are two reasons that providing food to container gardens is vital and even more important than doing the same for your in-ground plants.

First, the regular water necessary to keep container gardens from drying out flushes the nutrients out of the soil. And, second, the plants are not in a natural setting where they can send out roots in search of food—rather, they are completely at your mercy with regard to getting the nutrients they require.

Whether you choose to go with water-soluble or granular fertilizer depends on how you like to garden:

- Do you like to tend to your garden regularly? Do you have the time to mix up a batch of fertilizer on a weekly or biweekly basis and feed your

Right: These summer flowers have a short life cycle so feed them often to get the most blooming as possible.
Opposite: This wax begonia will flower continuously until first frost. That action requires a lot of energy, so feeding regularly will keep the blooms coming and the leafy growth full.

plants? If so, I would recommend a soluble choice, basically a powder form that you can mix with water in a watering can. As you water your plants, you'll be feeding them, too. This is my preferred method, but again, this only works if you have the time to complete this task with the required regularity.

- If you are able to tend to your plants only sporadically (and perhaps because of this have set up an irrigation system so that hand watering isn't required), I suggest a granular fertilizer that you can mix into the soil or scratch into its surface. Some granulated forms provide nourishment for up to six months, whereas less-expensive options are generally good for about two months. Feeding is only required through the growing season, so in most regions, this means ensuring your plants are fed April through September.

There are many formulations of fertilizer, so look for the one that best suits the plants you intend to feed, whether in a container or in your garden. If you are feeding your rhododendron and want to include the camellia as well, consider the fact that they're both spring-blooming broadleaf evergreens, so using the rhodo food for the camellia will be just fine. Always read the instructions for specific application rates.

Lastly, keep in mind that vegetables, herbs or other container-grown edibles are best served a regular helping of *organic* fertilizer. I only use organic on any produce that I bring to the kitchen table. These, too, are available in both granular and liquid forms.

How often should I feed my summer-blooming hanging baskets?

Surprisingly, there is not a short answer to this question…but, then again, when have any of my answers been short?

The best means of fertilizing your baskets is with a soluble fertilizer that's rich in the three major elements: nitrogen, phosphate and potash. For baskets, the most commonly recommended analysis is a soluble 15-30-15, which is very fast acting. It's important to know that, for the most part, plants will take what they need from the fertilizer provided and grow to the best of their ability. Having said that, particular elements within a fertilizer can force plants to do specific things. The higher phosphate content in the 15-30-15 will force flowering plants to send out more buds and blooms. Higher nitrogen content, as another example, will encourage lush green growth.

I highly recommend using fish fertilizer in conjunction with the soluble fertilizer, as it offers additional minerals and micro-nutrients. Fish fertilizer will also keep all of the foliage a lush dark green and assist with healthy growth early on.

Hanging gardens need conscientious feeding, because we water them so

Decorative hanging basket frames look nicer than plain plastic pots. Try an attractive wrought-iron basket like this one that can be used year after year.

frequently throughout summer, and this leaches much of the already-limited nutrition out of those little baskets stuffed with roots.

I have created a feeding chart that reflects fertilizer timing within the growing season and takes into consideration the increasing seasonal temperature as well as ever-changing light levels, as both affect a hanging basket's fertilizer needs.

This chart also takes into account that when plants are smaller they'll need a little less food a little more often. As they grow, it's best to increase the amount of food, because they have that much more bulk to maintain as they grow exponentially.

Sounds similar to my four boys, who are all in their teenage years or older and are at that bulk-maintenance stage where they get their exercise from pulling open the fridge door.

FOR A BOUNTY OF BLOOM…

The feeding of your planters and hanging baskets is crucial for healthy, lush plants with an abundance of bloom. You can choose the slow-release granular-fertilizer method, or my preference—admittedly a little more time-consuming—which is to follow the feeding chart below, using a combination of soluble 15-30-15 fertilizer and fish fertilizer. Please note that where both the soluble fertilizer and fish fertilizer are recommended, they should be combined into the same water volume as directed on the label. Enjoy a summer filled with colour!

	Fish Fertilizer:		Soluble Fertilizer:	
Month	**Frequency**	**Ratio**	**Frequency**	**Ratio**
March	Every watering	Half strength	Every week	Half strength
April	Every watering	Full strength	Every week	Half strength
May	Every week	Full strength	Every week	Full strength
June	Every week	Full strength	Every week	Full strength
July	Every week	Full strength	Every week	Full strength
August	Every week	Full strength	Every second week	Full strength
September	Every second week	Full strength	Every second week	Half strength

BULBS IN CONTAINERS

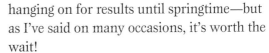
I love spring-blooming bulbs but only have pots to put them in. Should I do anything differently than I used to do when planting them in the ground? Also, how many can I stuff into one container?

A. Bulbs in containers look fantastic—when in bloom, they resemble a giant arranged bouquet in a vase! I highly recommend planting bulbs in containers…if you have patience. You'll need to plant in fall and will be hanging on for results until springtime—but as I've said on many occasions, it's worth the wait!

Planting bulbs in containers is similar to planting them in a flower bed, with adequate drainage being the biggest concern. Bulbs do not like sitting in waterlogged soil, so it is imperative that any excess moisture can escape through drain holes at the bottom of the pot (for more on this, see page 141).

When you're planting bulbs outside in a garden bed, place them at a depth of two times the height of the bulb itself. When you're planting in containers, I recommend that you place them an additional 30 percent deeper and at least 2 in. (5 cm) in from the sides of the pot. This will ensure protection from extreme cold, as container plantings are more exposed to the elements than bulbs or plants tucked directly into the ground. So if the bulb is 2 in. (5 cm) in height, you would plant it at a depth of 4 in. (10 cm) in a garden setting and about 6 in. (15 cm) in a pot.

Other than that, your success is pretty much guaranteed. And to get the maximum impact possible from your container garden, I suggest a layered planting of the bulbs. Basically, this is the process of planting bulbs on top of each other—what I like to call the "bunk-bed method."

A cute early-spring combination planter with mini daffodils, pansies, heather and evergreen euphorbia.

THE BUNK-BED METHOD OF LAYING BULBS IN A CONTAINER

1. Remove about 8 in. (20 cm) of soil from your container. Place that soil to the side for the moment.

Loosen the remaining soil in the container, stirring it up thoroughly at the same time.

Assuming the container is a minimum diameter of 18 in. (45 cm), mix ¼–½ cup (60–125 mL) of bulb food into the top layer of that mixed soil. If your container is smaller, reduce the amount accordingly.

2. Now you're ready for the big bulbs. Place large daffodils and tulip bulbs in clusters of five, keeping them about 1 in. (2.5 cm) away from each other. You can have as many clusters of different bulbs as you'd like. Use your imagination, and remember to put the taller growing bulbs in clusters near the back of the pot. Press them lightly into the soil.

3. Now take some of the previously removed soil and cover those bulbs so their tops have about an inch of soil covering them. Scratch about ½ cup (125 mL) of bulb food into the surface of the soil.

The bunk-bed method of layering bulbs in containers is an easy project to do with young children. It is fail proof and fun!

BEST FOR BULBS

Enjoy spring-blooming bulbs in containers on your patio—but for bulb longevity, dig them up and store them for the summer months (after the foliage has died back).

4. Next, place tiny bulbs, such as crocus, snowdrops, mini tulips or any of the other smaller-growing choices, in clusters of five on top of the soil you put on top of the larger bulbs. Again, you can place as many clusters of five bulbs as you'd like, spacing each bulb 1 in. (2.5 cm) apart.

5. Cover those bulbs with the remaining soil to within an inch of the top of the pot.

All that work and nothing to show for it…yet. But come February, those early-blooming smaller bulbs will shine, with a continuum of colour right through May.

Choosing bulbs for ongoing bloom time will provide a parade of colour, with each bulb type blooming after the next.

6. Finally, for a little life through fall and winter, plant winter pansies or other fall-blooming perennials in the top layer of soil. Surprisingly, all of the bulbs and plants will work in harmony, with each bulb finding its way to the surface without hindering another bulb or plant. The bunk-bed method of planting bulbs is simple and lets your designer personality surface as you plan for an ongoing show, fall through spring.

SUCCULENT PLANTERS

What's an easy-care plant for small pots on my deck? My husband and I like to travel and want something low maintenance.

Q.

A. I often tell people who are considering a pot for their patio that it's best to choose one that is not too small. An 18-in. (45-cm) diameter as a minimum size will usually ensure success—this holds enough soil to enable the container garden to go two or three days in the hot summer without being watered.

The 'Pia' (Hydrangea macrophylla 'Pia') is a hydrangea variety suitable for planting in a pot, since it grows to only 18 in. (45 cm).

There are exceptions, of course: if you have a large tree with a voluminous mass of foliage planted around it in a container, for example, three days might be a stretch. But, in general, the large-pot strategy works well to free you from daily maintenance of your container garden. Let's face it—the last thing you want to have at home is a pet when you don't have a pet! And a container that needs to be fed and watered and is restricting you from going away for the weekend might just as well be a pet. Planters and containers on your patio or deck are meant to enhance your life, not restrict it.

There are situations where a small planter is beautiful, such as on a small deck or outdoor table. And there is a great option for both little and large containers—one that has also been among the hottest planter trends of recent years. And that is succulents.

Yes, succulents. You might have in your mind a cactus, or jade plant, and wonder about the cold, as you don't want to have to bring it in during the winter. In fact, I'm talking about succulents that are hardy in cool climates and have many unique and attractive variations.

Above: This sedum 'Angelina' has great lime-green colour, grows very quickly and can be used as a groundcover, in hanging baskets or as filler in mixed planters.

Right: This sedum (Sempervivum) is a tough little trooper. Its preference for hot, dry conditions makes this perennial invaluable. It also spreads quickly and is winter hardy to zone 3.

There are dozens of different varieties of succulents, and most offer a significant enough bloom that they can be classified as a flowering plant. But even without a flower, they're extremely appealing, particularly in a smaller pot. The leaves can also be very colourful, as you can find reds, golds, greens, purples, near-black tones and more. They come in many shapes and sizes, from trailing, low-lying varieties to upright types that can grow to 2 ft. (60 cm). And you can create a lovely arrangement by mixing a number of different succulents in the same pot.

In the right soil and with good drainage, succulents in a pot can add a fabulous look to a small patio, and they can stay outdoors year round in regions with temperatures to zone 5 (-25F/-31C). Succulents don't require a rich soil and are not too particular about their growing conditions, aside from needing good drainage. Usually a mixture of 50 percent sand to soil will do the trick, assuming your container has the recommended number of drainage holes (see page 141).

The bonus benefit of succulents is that their fleshy leaves are like humps on a camel. They store water so that your succulent can wait six to ten days longer for water than a traditional flowering plant.

Outdoor succulents can be found in the perennial department of your local garden centre. I'm not going to even start listing their unpronounceable names but would recommend you check out the varieties appropriate for your climate.

VINES FOR BALCONIES

I live in an apartment and my balcony is looking a little bare. I love the scent of honeysuckle and would like to put a planter with a trellis on my balcony to double as a privacy screen. Would this work, or is there a better vine for this purpose?

Q.

A. Honeysuckle does not do well in pots for a couple of reasons. First, any stress from its roots drying would weaken the plant and make it susceptible to disease and insects. Second, the large number of leaves on a honeysuckle would be nearly impossible to keep hydrated during a summer dry spell, particularly in a windy location.

If you are looking for a vine and want fragrance, I would suggest trying a star jasmine (*Trachelospermum jasminoides*), as it is semi-evergreen with star-like, white blossoms all summer. If you live in zone 7 or warmer, it will survive through the winter with some protection. Bring it into a cool garage or

*The star jasmine (*Trachelospermum jasminoides*) is one of the longest-blooming vines, often flowering right up to Halloween. Added bonus: attractive deep-green, glossy foliage.*

very cool room, preferably with a window. Star jasmine grows very quickly and is worth a little effort to protect it over winter; otherwise, simply treat it as an annual, as the fragrance is wonderful all summer long.

HYDRANGEAS IN CONTAINERS

Do potted hydrangeas need to come inside for the winter? What's a year-round care strategy for them? I've been keeping them in the garage during the cold season.

Hydrangeas, as you are probably well aware, are a great container plant for the patio.

You'll also be happy to hear that winter care requires little effort. Now that you've moved your hydrangeas into the garage, you can lug them back outside again, because that is the best place for them over winter. In most zones, you can leave hydrangeas on your patio unprotected, as they are very cold hardy. Some are even just fine in zone 2, which can get as cold as -40! Ouch.

Every hydrangea has a different tolerance, and even though they all can handle a certain amount of cold, ensure that you have a variety appropriate for your climate. And if you are planting in a container, zone up! (See below.)

Also ensure that the containers they're planted in have adequate drainage; otherwise, your hydrangeas will be just fine, requiring the same maintenance and care as they would out in the garden.

Remember, too, that the best time to prune your hydrangea is in the fall (for more on this, see page 208).

Zone up those container plants

If you are planning to grow a perennial in a pot, zone up to ensure success! In a container, your plants have less protection from the cold than they would in the ground. So if you live in a zone 4, for example, I recommend that you select a plant variety that is hardy to zone 3.

CEDARS IN CONTAINERS

Would you recommend planting an emerald cedar in a container for a quick-growing screen for my patio garden?

Emerald cedars (*Thuja occidentalis* 'Smaragd') can definitely be grown in containers.

In fact, they are the perfect evergreen screen and are very easy to grow with little maintenance. Ensure that the containers you're considering are at least 20 in. (50 cm) wide by 20 in. (50 cm) deep, as emerald cedars grow a very dense and fibrous root system, and this requires space.

The biggest danger to potted emerald cedars is drying out over the summer, so you may wish to consider a dripper hose to ensure adequate, even moisture to the roots. The best means of feeding is a spring application of time-released granular hedge fertilizer that will offer ongoing nutrition for a period of four months.

Above: Favoured by designers for their wow impact in pots, these pink hydrangeas make a statement positioned in a front entrance.

TREES FOR CONTAINERS

I have a large south-facing deck on my condo. I love trees for their shade and beauty—can you suggest a few species that would do well in containers, be slow growing and tolerate full sun? And will these trees stay healthy in a container or will they eventually have to be transplanted into the ground?

The redbud (Cersis canadensis 'Forest Pansy') produces small pink flowers in early, early spring that literally cover the branches. Maroon coloured heart shaped leaves appear shortly after.

A. There are quite a number of trees that you could grow successfully in a container on your patio. If it's south facing, that is a benefit, as most shade trees prefer a sunny location.

Start with a good-sized container—as big as you can muster. A minimum container size is 26 in. (65 cm) across, but 30 in. (75 cm) or larger would be better still. That is big enough to contain a shade tree for many years and will provide pleasing proportions of tree size to pot. Most importantly, a large container ensures adequate root space and enough soil to retain water for at least a few days or so. Keep in mind that as the tree develops and produces more leaves, it will also use more moisture. Transplanting the tree down the

road is not a good option; you're better off planning for the appropriate size right from the start.

It is important to choose a tree that has a smaller overall long-term stature. Planting a mighty oak is not an option. Here are a few trees that have nice attributes and smaller overall mature size:

- **Japanese snowbell (*Styrax japonica*)** is a beautiful June bloomer—pink or white—that has an oval head easily maintained to an appropriate size. Dark-green summer leaves change to bright yellow in fall.
- **Redbud (*Cercis canadensis* 'Forest Pansy')** has beautiful, large, heart-shaped burgundy leaves. Deep-pink flowers are prolific in early spring on bare branches.
- **The maple family (*Acer palmatum*)** includes some of my favourite smaller-growing trees for locations with a little less sun. There are quite a number to choose from, with a good variety of leaf colours. They are very easy to grow and maintain to any width or height with a "V" shape from the pot up. Maples do best with some protection from full late-afternoon sun.

PALLET GARDENS

I know you advocate growing both vertical and horizontal gardens in recycled pallets—can you please tell me how to do this?

Q.

A. Previously disposed of in landfill sites or burn piles, pallets now have a new lease on life. Yards, walls and back alleys will be the new residence for pallets as people en masse use these growing vessels to produce their own crops. What were once platforms for the shipping of goods around the world are now becoming growing centres to help save the planet, as produce grown at home doesn't need to be shipped to us in carbon-spewing semi-trailers. Yes, the world is changing—one pallet at a time!

I have grown in both horizontal and vertical pallet gardens. Neither pallet garden style is meant for root crops, so don't expect beets and carrots to be part of this growing experience.

The best part about using a pallet is that they're usually free and often available at the back of almost any warehouse. I would suggest, though, that you ask before taking one, as some companies do reuse pallets, and you really don't want to be busted by a security camera and forever known as "the pallet thief"!

The horizontal pallet garden

Although it's really nothing more than a raised garden bed that can be placed in any sunny location, the horizontal pallet garden does offer some unique benefits compared to growing in the ground.

First, the wood slats absorb water and help to retain the moisture within the soil, so the roots of your veggies have some protection from drying out. And, second—and this is a big one—so far, no slugs have attempted to share my crops with me, which I believe is because the rough edges of the wood act as a deterrent.

I placed my horizontal pallet garden on a not-so-deep base of gravel near a children's play area in my yard that we don't really use any longer. Although you probably should cultivate the soil below where you place the pallet, this is not a requirement. As long as you provide water and nutrition, success with a mix of different crops is pretty much guaranteed.

The list of requirements is very small:

- Pallet (that was probably pretty obvious)
- Approximately 100 lb. (45 kg or 100 L) of a combination of soil, manure and soil conditioner
- Plants: I used three types of lettuce, a tomato, cucumber, zucchini, cilantro, basil and four strawberry plants. All have done relatively well; mind you, the strawberry plants became a little squished, as lettuce tends to overpower. Placing the strawberries on the edge would solve that.

The process of planting the horizontal pallet is quite simple:

1. Lay the pallet on the ground with the slats facing up. Although the open ends (where a forklift would place its forks) do not necessarily need to be closed or covered, doing so will keep the soil contained. Close in the ends by removing two slats from the underside of the pallet and nailing them over the open ends.

2. The next step is to fill the pallet with soil, making sure to pack it into every nook and cranny. Use gloves to avoid potential splinters from the wood pallet.

3. Once the pallet is filled with the soil mixture, plant your veggie seedlings. Water thoroughly. Enjoy your pallet garden year round by planting cold-tolerant edibles, such as kale and parsley. Or choose perennial herbs, such as rosemary and thyme, according to your zone.

The horizontal pallet garden is a easy and inexpensive way to make a raised garden.

The vertical pallet garden

Preparation and installation of the vertical pallet garden is more complicated and time-consuming than the horizontal version, but it's a very space-efficient way to grow an assortment of herbs and vegetables.

The first requirement is to determine where you can hang or place the vertical pallet, keeping in mind that a bright, sunny location is required. I hung my pallet garden from my fence. Surprisingly, it only adds an additional 12 in. (30 cm) of depth along the fenceline, so it does not encroach too dramatically on the yard.

There is also no reason why you couldn't stand the pallet upright, braced by a couple of posts on either side, or even have it standing and slightly tilted with back supports similar to an easel. I see this as a unique item for a patio that could also double as a visual or sound screen, as a soil-filled pallet is quite effective at reducing road noise or the sound of the neighbour's barking dog.

Although you might not think the pallet garden would be an attractive feature on a patio, once wrapped in black landscape fabric, the pallet becomes mute and simply a backdrop to the real focus—the plants.

The vertical pallet does require a little more effort and materials, but it is a fun and rewarding project.

The tools that you'll need for hanging a vertical pallet garden from a fence are:

- Pallet
- Two 3-in. eyehooks
- Two 3-in. regular hooks
- Hammer
- Handful of nails (sorry, I didn't count)
- Staple gun and box of stainless-steel staples
- 50-ft. (15-m) roll of landscape fabric
- One 4-ft. (120-cm) length of 1 × 4 lumber, which I simply took off another pallet
- Two 8–12-in. (20–30-cm) blocks of wood
- 100 lb. (45 kg or 100 L) of a combination of soil, manure and soil conditioner (basically a very fine composted bark material to ensure the soil within the pallet is quite porous so that water can move quickly through it to the plant material at the base of the pallet. Porous soil will ensure even and thorough water and fertilizer distribution.
- 160-ft. (50-m) roll of nylon string or jute (optional, see step 5)
- Sharp knife

The process of building the vertical pallet garden, including installing it on the fence and planting it up, took me less than two hours. And the cost of all of the required materials including plants—some of which were herbs and so a little more expensive than vegetables—was eighty dollars. The pallet was free. Half the cost was for soil, so if you can use some of your own compost, this would reduce the total quite dramatically.

Here are the steps I took to build my vertical pallet garden:

1. Position the pallet on the ground with the bottom facing up, and crisscross (doubling up) the landscape fabric over the back of it—and over what will become the bottom, when hung. You'll have to decide which end is the top and which is the bottom of the garden, but it shouldn't matter which arrangement you choose. I used lots of staples to ensure the fabric was securely in place, as the heavy soil will put pressure on the back of the pallet (and having the fabric give way mid season would be very disappointing and, needless to say, messy). Ensure the base of the pallet is securely covered by fabric as well, to prevent soil from leaching out of cracks once you install the 1 x 4 to seal the bottom.

2. Next, secure that 4-ft. (120-cm) 1 x 4 along the base of the pallet (where a forklift's prongs would normally slide in). You can nail into the 2 x 4 on either side of the pallet (which all the other slats are also nailed into). You'll be covering up the landscape fabric you had already put in place at the base of the pallet.

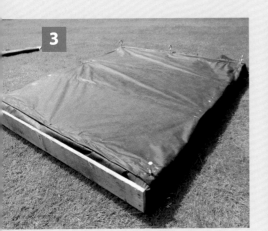

3. Now install the eyehooks—the connection between the pallet and the fence—on both sides of the top of the backside of the pallet (the side you placed the landscape fabric on). These two eyehooks will attach to the regular hooks you'll install into the top 2 x 4 on the fence (usually just below the common lattice top). Ensure that you measure the distance between the two eyehooks on the pallet and install the two regular hooks at exactly the same distance apart on the fence so that they can easily clip into the eyehooks.

4. Finally, before hanging the pallet on the fence, nail the two 8–12-in. (20–30-cm) blocks of wood onto the two bottom back corners of the base of the pallet. These blocks are to prevent the pallet from leaning against the fence panels on an angle, and will instead hold the pallet in a standing upright position on the fence. Yay, you can hang up your pallet garden now!

5. Now we can get to the fun part. Cut three strips of landscape fabric 5 ft. (1.5 m) long. Place the landscape fabric across the front bottom of the pallet, stapling just the bottom of the fabric to the bottom board. Fill the inside-bottom of the pallet with soil up to the first opening, and lay plants on this soil. Each plant should be on its side with roots lying on soil just inside the pallet, with stems and foliage protruding outside the pallet boards.

I wanted to take advantage of the space along the fence panels on either side of the frame to allow my tomatoes, cucumbers and zucchini to grow along string-lines attached to the pallet, stretched approximately 6.5 ft. (2 m) horizontally along the fence to the next post. I simply hammered a nail in along the edge of the pallet, attached a string and stretched it to another nail hammered into the next fence post. This gave me a sturdy string-line that could support weighty tomatoes, cucumbers and zucchini. Placement of plants is important if you intend to do the same—heavy-cropping plants should be planted just inside either side of the pallet so that they can easily be trained to grow along a string-line right next to them outside the pallet edge. I also planted a 'tumbler' tomato at the bottom centre to hang below the pallet. Overall, you can expect at least a 10-ft. (3-m) width of plant material from your 4-ft. (120-cm) pallet, with the plants sprawling on either side and along the string-lines.

6. Now that you have the bottom row of plants placed, pull the fabric up over it. With a sharp knife, slice through the fabric and gently pull the small seedlings through. Staple the fabric into the next slat above each plant that has just been pulled through, and continue along the row until you've pulled every seedling through a slice in the fabric. Now, punch a few extra staples in for good measure to hold everything tight to the pallet.

7. Push soil into the next slat. It will fall into the pallet and cover the roots of the vegetable and herb plants below. Pack firmly as you go.

8. Once you've added soil to the top of the next pallet slat, repeat the same steps as you did for the bottom row of vegetable and herb plants—placing the fabric, positioning the plants with their roots sideways and pulling the vegetables and herbs through—working your way up to the top slat.

And a tip: When I completed the planting of the top row of vegetables and herbs, I stapled and pulled the plants through, as I did with all of the others below them, but was left with about 2 ft. (60 cm) of fabric. I tucked this extra fabric into the inside of the top of the pallet, across the top of the soil covering the roots of the top row of plants, and up the back side of the

Two weeks later and an attractive addition to the fence.

inside of the pallet. This created a trough of landscape cloth about 4 in. (10 cm) deep across the pallet top. I purposely did not fill the top slat of the pallet with soil; instead, I wanted to use it as a reservoir for water, which allowed the water to slowly trickle into the soil right down to the bottom row of plants.

These are the edibles that worked very well in my vertical pallet garden:

VEGETABLES

- 'Roma' tomato
- 'Sweet 100' tomato
- 'Tumbler' tomato
- Three 'Sweet Success' cucumber
- Seven 'Tri Star' strawberry
- 'New Zealand' spinach
- Zucchini
- Three kale
- Five leaf lettuce

HERBS

- Greek oregano
- Golden oregano
- Creeping thyme
- Variegated thyme
- Creeping rosemary
- Large-leaf basil
- Tricolour sage
- Cilantro
- English mint

Opposite:
Quick lawn facts:
• Lawns improve air quality by trapping dust and other airborne particles
• Lawns are the best natural surface to trap and store rainwater
• Lawns reduce soil erosion
• Lawns absorb carbon dioxide and release oxygen
• Lawns act as nature's air conditioner by cooling the air

Lawns & Groundcovers

In this section, I hope to give you some insight into green. No, not that "green"! I'm talking about the expanse of green that resides around your flower beds—your lawn.

Since it's often the biggest part of the landscape, keeping the lawn healthy and weed-free goes a long way toward keeping a yard looking fresh and tidy. I like to compare the lawn to the matting around a picture in a frame, with a tight-cropped border and warm complementary colour that draws the eye to the garden and other features.

I believe lawns get a bad rap and disagree with those who say they are unnecessary. Plus, they *can* be considered "green": lawns actually help to cool the earth, filter rain, prevent excessive water runoff and purify the air. Keep it organic and use a push mower or electric version instead of a gas-guzzler, and you're all the greener. And those clippings make an excellent water-saving mulch and are also great for the compost heap.

Yes, it does take a bit of water to keep it the colour green during the summer months, but that's how we get to benefit from all a lawn has to offer. Or, if you're in an area where there are watering restrictions, you might not be able to enjoy a lush lawn all summer long, but like a loyal friend, it will return in good spirits with the arrival of the fall rains.

Through the following questions and answers, you will gain insight into what makes a lawn grow, plus how to control weeds and other pests and problems…and you will get the answer to that age-old question, "When should I lime?" From now on, it will be your side of the fence where the grass is greener.

Q. *When is the best time to start a lawn, and is sowing from seed better than using sod or turf?*

A. The time to start seed can vary depending on where you live, but the general rule is that April is the start of the sowing season, though there is a large window for planting that lasts right through June. Another good sowing season for lawns is September through early October, when the earth is warm and seed germinates quickly, with relatively fast growth because of the still-strong light levels.

I personally like a lawn from seed rather than sod or turf, as this provides more options for matching the choice of grass to particular conditions. Every seed variety adapts differently to varying soil conditions and environments, so a blend has a stronger chance of offering a good end result.

A mix of both annual and perennial grasses is particularly valuable for regions that have a milder climate, as the perennial seed can provide a green lawn year round. And although it goes dormant in the winter, it still remains green.

Whether you choose sod or seed, you'll want to prepare your lawn-dedicated area well to enjoy a lush-looking expanse of grass in the not-too-distant future. Here's what to do:

1. Lay down a solid base of topsoil: 4–6 in. (10–15 cm) will provide enough depth for a healthy lawn. Pay a little extra attention to the soil alongside sidewalks and driveways. I recommend a minimum depth of 6 in. (15 cm) in those areas, because cement and pavement heat up in summer and any lawn abutting those areas will dry out faster. An additional 2 in. (5 cm) or more of soil will help the lawn grow a deeper and more resilient root system. More soil and more depth means more available moisture for the lawn to cool itself down.

2. Before seeding, ensure your grade is as level as possible but with a slight slope away from the home if possible to encourage excess water from heavy or continual rainfall to flow in the right direction.

Pay particular attention to preparing a level surface for your new lawn. A level lawn not only looks more appealing but is also safer for walking and playing.

3. Next, compress the soil. For larger areas, a roller is the best means to ensure it is firmly packed. After rolling the soil, it is also much easier to see where there are low or high spots. Level out any areas of concern and then complete a second rolling in another direction.

4. The next step is to scratch or scuff the soil's surface. You may want to do this in sections so that you can "scuff, sow and go." The intent here is to have the seed fall on the scuffed soil, rather than firm rolled soil, or even your hard footprint, to allow for maximum germination.

5. Scatter the seed liberally and evenly. For the average yard, this is done most easily and with the most control when applied by hand. Coverage information will be on the grass-seed package.

6. Once the seed is distributed, you can roll the entire sown area again. But, this time, take the water out of the roller. The purpose of this rolling is to gently bind the seed with the soil; this will help to keep the seed from drying out. Take heart…we're almost done.

7. I suggest now placing a thin layer of soil or compost over top of the seed—again, best done by hand—to hide it from birds and also ensure it doesn't dry out if the sun starts shining. A little coating of soil over top of the freshly laid seed will help it to germinate even faster. Dark in colour, soil will absorb the sun's heat, which seeds need to sprout. This is of particular importance in the early spring, when the cold of winter is slowly dissipating from the ground. Think of the after-winter earth as an ice cube. Place your hand just a couple of centimetres above a cube and you'll feel the cold escaping into the warmer surroundings. It could be temperate outside, but the cool earth is preventing the soil from warming enough to germinate the grass seed. A small amount of soil will absorb the heat from the sun and warm up the seed. Once the seed has germinated and begun growing, the cooler temperatures will not negatively affect your new lawn.

8. However, once germinated, the seed must remain just slightly moist. Regular waterings in short intervals (every four hours) during the day for five to ten minutes are ideal. Then, as the lawn starts to grow, gradually reduce the frequency and increase the volume. If you're lucky, rain will help with the watering workload and you may not need to bother irrigating. But, simply stated, you don't ever want the newly germinated grass seed to go dry, especially not before you have completed your first couple of cuts.

9. Use a lawn-starter fertilizer applied by a spreader as your final step. Most commercial soils contain very little nutrition, and your new lawn is going to be hungry as it starts growing.

10. You're done! Enjoy that luxurious new lawn.

My mission this spring/summer is to obtain a perfect lawn. Is it important to remove ruts and dips from my existing grass first?

A. The route to a perfect lawn does start with ensuring it is free of dips. Any rut or depression will collect water, which will prevent air circulation in the soil, causing lawn roots to rot and soil to sour.

Your best bet is to bring in topsoil and spread it over the entire lawn. Generally, a top dressing of soil on an existing lawn will build up a better base for it to grow in. I recommend ½ in. (1 cm) one to two times per year, in spring and fall. Plus, increased soil will help to retain moisture during the dry summer months and also hold on to nutrients the lawn can draw from. Your lawn will also grow a stronger root system, which makes it more durable.

In some areas, the added soil may be too thick for your existing lawn to grow through. Placing 2 in. (5 cm), or any amount that would hide all the green of the grass, would be enough to smother the lawn and kill it. In those spots, simply scratch the top of the earth and reseed (as per the previous question). I suggest placing a thin layer of soil over the seed to make it less obvious to foraging birds and to ensure it doesn't dry out.

Regular waterings in short intervals (every four hours) during the day for five to ten minutes are ideal. Then, as the lawn starts to grow, gradually reduce the frequency and increase the volume.

And don't forget the food. Lawns grow quite steadily, as we well know from the required weekly mowing, so nutrition is imperative. For more on feeding your lawn, see page 175.

One of the greatest joys for a kid is to run around barefoot on the lawn! To me, this picture simply says: happy.

Q. *How can I eliminate the moss that keeps taking over my lawn?*

A. Moss loves an acidic soil and will thrive in an almost invasive fashion, overpowering and destroying lawns. Although moss is green and can look unassuming, it doesn't replace a lawn as it has no formal root system and will tear up easily and brown out when dry. It can be more of a detriment than a benefit.

Two essential ingredients applied annually—moss killer and lime—will eliminate moss from your lawn. Both are safe to use around pets and kids. Although this is usually done in the spring, two applications of lime a year are a good idea in rainy, temperate climates. It doesn't matter what order they are applied in, but you do need about 24 hours of dry weather after you apply the moss killer for it to thoroughly do its job. The moss should be moist before application, though, so if it's not damp from dew or previous rainfall, give it a light sprinkling first.

Apply moss killer on a guaranteed dry day anytime March through June, and you will see the moss start to die within hours. After at least 48 hours, rake out as much of the blackened moss as possible; you can put it in the compost box if you wish, though it's probably better buried in a shallow hole.

If you have a moss problem and you haven't limed yet this year, then do

Little-known moss facts:
- *Did you know moss was used for dressing wounds in World War I?*
- *Reindeer eat moss because it has a chemical that keeps their blood warm.*
- *Moss will grow on the east, west and south sides of trees.*

so now no matter what time of year it is with a fast-acting lime. This will increase the soil pH and discourage moss from returning. Be very generous with the lime. And don't forget to apply it to your flower beds and vegetable gardens, but skip your cedars, rhododendrons, azaleas, camellias and potato patch (for more on this, see page 115).

The majority of the moss will be controlled in one application, but you might want to consider a second course of moss killer after about a month to completely eliminate it.

As traditional moss killer is iron-based, sweep any overspray granules off of sidewalks and driveways to avoid leaving a rusty stain. You can also buy all-natural liquid forms that can be sprayed on.

For a monthly schedule of lawn maintenance, see below.

Could you provide me with a year-round guide of what do, and when, for lawns? **Q.**

A. Here's a quick guide to annual care for your lawn:
February: For regions with chronically low pH, apply prilled lime (a pelletized form of lime) to increase soil pH and prevent moss from invading (read more about this on page 174).

Although watering a lawn is important, only twice a week for about a half an hour is necessary to keep it healthy.

March: Apply a spring start-up lawn fertilizer (following the moss killer, if it was used). This feeding is best done immediately after power raking, if that is necessary

March/April: Apply moss killer if necessary (read more about this on page 170).

March/April: Aerate. Although this is a worthy and beneficial project to complete annually, it could be done every second year.

March/April: Power rake if necessary to eliminate dead moss and thatch buildup (see page 180). There are specific long-handled rakes for the manual method, or you can purchase a thatch blade from your garden centre to attach to the base of your lawn mower, or you can rent a professional power rake. There are also professionals you can hire to do this for you.

May: Apply slow-release high-nitrogen fertilizer. All fertilizers should be applied with a wheeled fertilizer spreader or a hand fertilizer spreader.

May–September: Watering of the lawn is only required twice a week (check to see if you have watering restrictions and specific allowable watering days in your area). Approximately 30 minutes on both days is all that should be required to keep your lawn green through the hot summer months.

July: For a continued lush lawn, apply a second application of a slow-release high-nitrogen lawn fertilizer. This would only be in the case of those who want to keep their lawn green over the summer months. Water restrictions should not affect your ability to keep a lawn green over the summer, as most jurisdictions with water restrictions still allow two watering days per week—more than enough to keep a lawn green. A July application of slow-release lawn fertilizer will ensure it also remains lush. There are areas that do struggle through severe summer water shortages and where lawn watering is banned completely. For those who are faced with this situation or prefer not to water the grass at all, the result will be a brown lawn, assuming it's a dry summer. Come the rains of fall, though, the lawn will return to its green glory.

Late September: Apply fall and winter lawn fertilizer, which contains more phosphate and potash than nitrogen. Some fall nutrition will prepare your lawn for winter and assist in root growth that will make it sturdier. A winter fertilizer will also strengthen your lawn and make it more tolerant of rain, snow and cold.

October: Apply moss killer if necessary.

October: Apply a second application of prilled lime

October/November: Ensure all leaves are raked off the lawn as soon as possible.

November–February: Avoid walking on the lawn wherever you can.

SOIL AMENDMENTS FOR LAWNS

How important is lime for my lawn?

Q.

A. Lime can be a vitally important addition to your lawn—actually for the soil below it—but only if the pH is low.

First, I should explain that whether soil is acid or alkaline relates to the pH scale. And that managing the pH of soil is very similar to adjusting the pH of a hot tub. A balanced pH in a hot tub is vitally important to ensure all the chemicals work as they are supposed to. A similar imbalance can occur in our soil, if the pH becomes too high or low. Nutrition can get locked in the soil and become unavailable to plants, which will affect whether a plant responds to whatever nourishment you're providing.

A mossy lawn may be caused by a low pH balance, which you can correct by using lime.

You need to do a pH test to see whether it is necessary for you to add lime to your lawn. You can pick up a vial test from a local garden centre. Or you can choose a pH instrument that has a probe that measures the pH when inserted into the soil below your lawn. Neither of these pH-testing techniques is expensive, and both can be used to benefit your garden over and over again for years.

As there is seldom a need to lower the pH of soil, let me give you advice on how to raise it. One of the best and most affordable ways to increase the pH of soil is by adding lime. Lime is an organic material that can be applied to your lawn and garden as you would a fertilizer, by simply spreading by hand or, better still, with a spreader to ensure even distribution. Although there are different types of lime available, I highly recommend you use a dolomite-lime form. You can purchase lime in a powder or a prilled (pellet) form that is easier to use and less messy.

Heather loves acidic soil.

I live in a region where the soil is very acidic. This is not healthy for plants that don't like acidic soil. Okay, that sounded like I was being smart, but not everyone knows that some plants like a slightly acidic soil, whereas others prefer it to be a little more alkaline.

Where excessive annual rainfall creates a chronically low soil pH, the addition of lime to raise the pH to neutral is required at least annually. I tell people who live in my area that, without even testing, they need to lime annually to balance the soil pH to ensure success.

Another common reason those of us in regions with a low pH apply lime annually is to help prevent moss from accumulating in our lawns (for more on this, see page 170). Raising the pH of the soil with lime won't kill existing moss but will inhibit it from growing and thriving.

Lime is not always fast acting, so don't expect instant results. For those in areas with high rainfall, it's best to plan on an annual application to lawns, flower beds and vegetable gardens (but not to cedars, rhododendrons, azaleas, camellias or potatoes). Liming at least once annually is a perfect example of the old saying "Prevention is the best medicine."

Q. I traditionally feed my lawn in spring, and then nothing else. It's not as green and healthy as other lawns on my block, though—should I be feeding it more often?

A. A lawn can be an integral part of your yard, particularly if there are kids or pets in your household. Or if you have a horse.

Although a lawn does require regular maintenance (see page 171), in my opinion, fertilizer is the key to creating a lush, healthy lawn. I recommend that you fertilize it at least two, preferably three, and ultimately four, times a year—but not always with the same product.

People sometimes think that when they throw down fertilizer on a lawn it's going to grow like crazy. Not true. This used to be the case when only the inexpensive single-source nitrogen fertilizers were available, but now this has changed with advanced formulations and the use of different sources of nitrogen, along with nitrogen coatings. Sulphur-coated urea or other

A healthy lawn can enhance a flower bed like great matting around a picture.

nitrogen-coating technologies are unique in that manufacturers glaze a certain percentage of the nitrogen granules in the fertilizer. I like to call it "Smartie coating"—melts in your lawn, not in your hand. The coated nitrogen granules slowly break down over an extended period, offering long-term feeding that is so much better for your lawn than the old-fashioned formulas.

A lawn—or any plant, for that matter—that gets nutrition on a regular basis is going to be that much healthier, insect and disease resistant, and structurally stronger. It's similar to you or me. Regular nutrition keeps us healthy. It's not good for your health to feed you a turkey dinner and then tell you that there will be nothing else for you to eat for a week. Fertilizers that slowly release nutrition are one of the best improvements in the horticultural industry over the past few decades.

Early spring

A lawn that gets nutrition on a regular basis is going to be healthy, insect and disease resistant and structurally strong.

So let's start with spring. Coming out of winter, light levels are increasing, temperatures are rising and your lawn is hungry. Since it's still relatively cool, you won't require the slow-release nitrogen fertilizer yet, as nitrogen already breaks down slowly in cool temperatures. Look for a fertilizer with a ratio of 3-1-2. A common spring lawn fertilizer is 13-5-7, which is close to that ratio. This can be applied any time March through May.

May through July

Your second or possibly third fertilizing period is sometime in late May through July. Consider the colour of your lawn to gauge when you might want to feed it. Dark green suggests your lawn is healthy and actively growing, but a fade to bright green indicates it's time to give it some fertilizer. There is no right or wrong here, and if you're too early with the next feed, you'll do no harm and, in fact, only good, because the next product I recommend is a slow-release lawn food (with a ratio of 4-1-2). So a 24-6-12 lawn fertilizer would be appropriate for your summer application, as long as there is at least 50 percent slow-release nitrogen in the formula. Lawns feed quite aggressively through summer, as they are actively growing, so two applications of the slow-release fertilizer might be necessary to keep your lawn lush and dark green. Space those feedings approximately two months apart.

Fall and into winter

Finally, fall and winter nutrition helps, too. Higher potash is a requirement for the winter lawn, and 2-1-4 is the appropriate food ratio to strengthen and prepare your lawn for the cold and dark winter months ahead. Do your fall application September through October.

LAWN PROBLEMS

How do I eliminate mushrooms from my lawn?

Q.

A. Mushrooms in the lawn may be unsightly, but the good news is that they don't do any damage.

Mushrooms can only grow from decaying material under the earth, and they set spores and seed to continue their species. There is no product to eliminate them, nor does there need to be. The best method of control is the ol' football technique. Simply kick them down before they get too big and prior to their setting spores. This should end the mushroom run and send you to the Spores Hall of Fame (sorry).

Mushrooms can be found in fairy tales, folktales, folk remedies and superstitions. In Welsh lore, mushrooms are fairy food, but you should keep the grocery store as your culinary source.

Q. Is there an organic method to get rid of dandelions?

A. Dandelions—as cute and happy as they might look with their bright-yellow flowers—can actually become a menace, as the flower transforms into a globe of fluffy seed pods ready to fly off and invade other parts of your lawn and garden.

The Swiss came up with the first and best all-natural and organic method of eliminating dandelions from a lawn. It's called the Swiss Army knife. Although I'm not sure this was their intent at the time, I have eliminated thousands of dandelions in my day, all because I carry this knife in my pocket at all times. It also gets used time and time again for pruning and plucking. The technique I use for controlling dandelions with my Swiss Army knife is to simply cut the dandelion top off as far below the surface of the lawn as the knife will reach. The top gives way easily for disposal, and your lawn will quickly fill in the bare spot. If the flower has not transformed into seed and is still its sunny self, you can simply compost the whole thing. If they are seedy, however, it's best not to take a chance, so either bury them deeply or put them out with the waste recycling curbside.

The dandelion has what is known as a taproot. That's a root that looks almost like a small carrot and can grow several inches deep into the soil.

Little-known dandelion facts:
• Originally from Asia, dandelions have been in Canada since at least the 1700s
• Seeds can be carried on the wind for up to 5 miles (8 km)
• 93 different insects use dandelion pollen as food
• Dandelions have one of the longest flowering seasons of any plant

Obviously, when you cut that dandelion out of your lawn, some of this deep root will be left behind. Depending on the time of year, that taproot will either simply die, as it won't have the energy to send out new growth, or it will send out new growth and a two-headed dandelion will emerge. This is not because it has transformed into an alien lawn invader but is actually quite a normal reaction that plants can have when the central leader is removed. After a couple of weeks, if you notice two smaller shoots growing from where you've cut the mother dandelion, simply cut it off again. After a second slicing, the remaining taproot will not have the energy to send out shoots for a third time.

That's the way to take the roar out of the dandelion.

Left: Keep on top of dandelion control. Let your guard down for a few weeks and they can quickly get out of hand. Jay Shaw photo
Right: Dive in with a Swiss Army knife! Jay Shaw photo

Q. *I have lots of dead grass at the base of my lawn, and this is making it look quite unpleasant. Is this thatch? How do I get rid of this problem?*

A. Yes, what you have is thatch, the buildup of dead grass from the past year, or years.

To explain, a lawn is ideally composed of both annual and perennial grasses.

Perennial grasses are the less vigorous of the two through summer but are just as their name suggests—perennial. They remain year round, offering a green base throughout winter (unless the cold temperatures take their toll and turn them temporarily brown), and do not leave behind much in the way of thatch.

Annual grasses are vigorous in the warm weather, growing green and lush throughout the summer. It's the grass we curse when we have to go out and mow it at least once a week. It's the grass that we swear we're going to pave over. It's the grass that fills up the compost box, leaving our kitchen scraps to rot and smell just outside our back door as we wait for the clippings to break down…well, you get the idea. It also offers that nice pillowy grass we so enjoy. Ahhh, I hear a picnic calling.

Annual grasses die in the winter and leave behind seeds to ensure a healthy return the following summer. They also leave behind remnants, basically dead grass, or "thatch."

Usually, the thatch buildup from one growing season of annual grasses will not prevent you from having a lush green lawn the following year. Too much thatch, however, and it will start to smother the soil and create competition for your lawn.

How much is too much thatch? Basically, if you can look down at your lawn in April and see as much brown as green, you have too much thatch.

There are three efficient ways to eliminate this problem from your yard:

1. The first option is the "sweat-and-tears method." Simply rake it out with either a stiff-tined rake or a specific moss and thatch rake. Okay, "simply" might not be the appropriate word, but raking it out is an option.

2. Purchase from your local garden centre an attachment that hooks up to the bottom of your lawn mower. Remove your lawn-mower blade, install the thatching blade and run your mower over the lawn as if you were cutting it. The tines that are attached to this blade will rip any thatch from your lawn to the extent that you'd think you were on a baler in the Prairies—it will pull out more than you would have ever suspected was there. The thought "I could feed a small hobby farm's worth of horses and cattle for a year" might come to mind!

3. Lastly, you can rent—from pretty much any tool-rental shop—a thatching machine or what's commonly referred to as a power rake. This will also tear any thatch right out of your lawn. You may wish to have about a dozen of those paper garden recycling bags on hand, because there will be way too much debris for the average compost box.

No matter which method you choose, your lawn will thank you. You will invigorate it, giving it the opportunity to grow lush and thick once again. This is the time when I also recommend you apply a high-nitrogen slow-

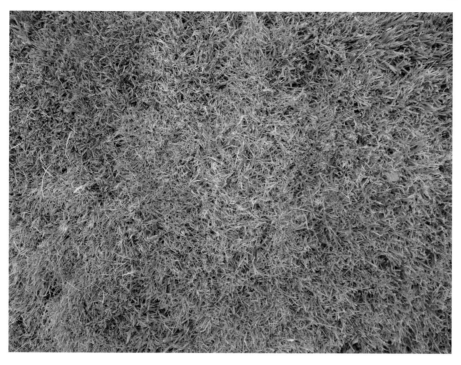

Rid your lawn of thatch to rejuvenate it and allow it to "breathe again."

release fertilizer to power start your turf, something in the neighbourhood of a 13-5-7.

And, just in case you need a little reassurance after the job…your thorough de-thatching might leave you thinking you've torn up your lawn and made things worse, but what you've actually done is made light and air available to roots that are alive and well—and will start growing immediately after the removal of their competition.

What can I do about the European chafer grubs that have raccoons tearing up (and destroying) my lawn?

A. The chafer beetle is a very large grub found under the surface of your lawn at certain times of year—and it is quite a delicacy for crows, raccoons and skunks, which will rip through turf to get to them. The majority of lawn damage related to this chafer-fuelled feeding frenzy happens in early spring and can be compared to the results of a rototiller churning through your grass.

To repair the damage, pack your lawn down, levelling any pitting with fresh soil and sand, and reseed with a quality lawn seed. Then feed the repaired patches a slow-release lawn fertilizer.

To prevent future chafer-beetle damage, consider a mid-summer application of nematodes, available from your local garden centre. Nematodes are a microscopic wormy-looking creature that when released in water and applied to your lawn (and we're talking about millions of them per package), will search out and destroy any newly hatched chafer beetle larvae.

A year in the life of a chafer beetle...

The European chafer beetle completes its life cycle in one year. Eggs hatch around mid July, and the grubs molt twice over eight weeks. The mature grubs are well adapted to cool, moist conditions and feed on the roots of your lawn all fall. During the winter, they dig down during periods of freezing conditions but otherwise remain within 2 in. (5 cm) of the surface. They feed in the spring until April, when they become pupae. Adults emerge in late May, fly to nearby deciduous trees to mate and feed, and then females deposit up to fifty eggs each—usually in one of the nice nearby lawns.

The European chafer beetle was first identified in New Westminster in 2001 and has since spread to Burnaby and other Lower Mainland communities.

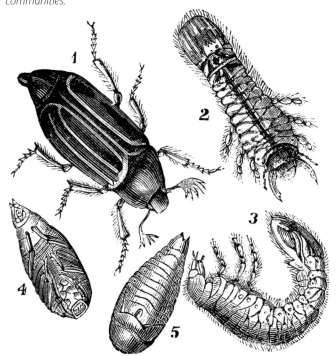

The larval stage in the life cycle of the chafer, usually mid summer, is when birds and raccoons will tear up your lawn.

Eggs hatch during summer and begin to feed on the fibrous roots of grass. By fall, they are fat grubs, and wildlife begin to feed on them.

LAWN ALTERNATIVES

Help! Since the chafer beetle reached our neighbourhood, our lawn has been a disaster—what groundcover can we plant to replace it?

Q.

A. Moss, weeds, thatch and now chafer beetle can all offer a good reason to switch your green lawn patch to a green groundcover patch, particularly if you're dealing with a small space.

The female chafer beetle particularly likes a lawn as a place to deposit eggs, as it is a favourable host for larvae to grow through to their emergence the following year as adults. The chafer beetle—and the resulting damage to lawns caused by birds, raccoons and other creatures foraging for grubs—has some folks looking for alternatives to grass. Here are some chafer-resistant alternatives to a lawn, offering flowers, colour and fragrance, without sacrificing the option of light foot traffic:

- **Brass buttons (*Leptinella squalida*):** My favourite is the bronze-leaved variety 'Platt's Black'. Dark green is also available. This is probably the lowest growing (maximum of 2 in./5 cm) of all of my recommendations and the best groundcover for areas with heavy foot traffic. Brass buttons have a unique leaf structure, grow very densely to ensure thorough coverage of an area and offer great weed suppression. They bloom June through July with either yellow or white blossoms and tolerate sun to part shade. Hardy to zone 5.
- **Woolly thyme (*Thymus pseudolanuginosus*):** Another beautiful creeping groundcover, with masses of hairy, green miniature leaves and an abundance of pink blossoms in June and July. Grows to a maximum of 2 in. (5 cm) and prefers poor, dry, rocky soil in a sunny location. You'll enjoy the herbal thyme fragrance when you walk on it, but only light foot traffic is tolerated by this relatively fast-growing, deer-proof evergreen option. Hardy to zone 5.
- **Creeping chamomile or Roman chamomile (*Chamaemelum nobile*):** Also a popular herb that can handle light foot traffic, it grows 4–6 in. (10–15 cm) in preferred sun or part-shady areas. The attractive ferny leaves move gently in a breeze and offer a light herbal fragrance. Enjoy white, daisy-like flowers in June and July. Mow or shear after blooming. Hardy to zone 4.

Clover in small quantities does not hinder a lawn's performance, but the blossoms can attract bees. Removal by hand can be tedious but beneficial to control its invasive nature.

- **Dutch white clover (*Trifolium repens*):** White clover—yes, just like the clover we try to eliminate from our lawns—is normally sown by seed, and a large area can be planted very affordably. It is relatively low growing, to 4–6 in. (10–15 cm), and can tolerate light foot traffic. It grows well in shade or full sun, is drought tolerant and stays green through the hottest part of the summer. The white blossoms in a ball shape above the leaves are continual May through September but can attract bees. Mowing may be necessary once or twice throughout the growing season but is not imperative. Hardy to zone 4.

- **Bugleweed (*Ajuga reptans*):** This is a spectacular groundcover for many reasons. First, it is evergreen, so there is no down time, plus it's available in a few different leaf colours and the variegated variety is a standout. All varieties bloom showy purple flowers on a spike May through June and early July. It only tolerates very light foot traffic, as the average height is around 1 ft. (30 cm). It's great for a shady, moist area though, as it prefers a wet environment. Hardy to zone 3.

- **Japanese spurge (*Pachysandra terminalis*):** This is another beautiful full groundcover. It prefers a moist area and can tolerate shade to full sun. In bright sun, the lush dark-green foliage can fade marginally. It also blooms tiny white flowers in March and April and is a hardy and durable groundcover. Japanese spurge can tolerate some foot traffic, but this is not recommended, as the stems can grow 1–2 ft. (30–60 cm) and would bend and break with any amount of traffic. Although it recovers quickly, the patch would look trampled for a period. Hardy to zone 4.

🪴 **Creeping thyme (*Thymus*):** This is a very sturdy, low-growing ever-green groundcover barely 1 in. (2.5 cm) high that prefers a sunny location with good drainage. It tolerates light foot traffic and has deep-pink flowers early through mid summer. Hardy to zone 2.

🪴 **Scotch moss (*Sagina subulata aurea*) or Irish moss (*Sagina subulata*):** Some might think that I'm out of my mind recommending moss, but both Scotch and Irish moss are different from what so many people try to eliminate from their gardens and, more particularly, from their lawns. Scotch moss is a bright neon-yellow, whereas Irish moss is more of a shamrock green. Both prefer a sunny location but can tolerate light shade. Although the blooms are very tiny, they will flower sporadically late spring through summer. They both can handle light foot traffic and although they have different common names, they are of the same family and require similar growing conditions and care. Hardy to zone 3.

Q. *I can't seem to have success with a lawn in a shady spot of my yard, no matter what I've tried. Can you recommend some plants or a groundcover that would work as a substitute?*

A. Without a doubt, growing a lawn in a shady location is more difficult than growing one in a sunny spot.

Before you go the route of tearing up your lawn and planting groundcovers, you might want to first try a shade-loving grass seed. This can make all the difference between success and failure. Remember the old saying "Right plant, right place"—this relates to a lawn as well. Not all grasses are the same. They might all look relatively similar, but there are thousands of different varieties of grass seed.

You need a grass that enjoys a shady area, or even tolerates shade. One of the more common shade-loving grass-seed varieties is *Poa trivialis*, or rough-stalk bluegrass. Look for this seed in the blend you choose. Or you may find a blend specifically labelled for shade.

Assuming, however, that your comment "no matter what I've tried" means you've already attempted the shade-grass route, there are some groundcover perennials that may work well to fill in your shady spot. But, just to be clear, there is no groundcover I can recommend that completely duplicates a lawn. So if you're looking for something that you can have your

Low groundcovers surround stepping stones at the foot of this colourful rock garden. This well-thought-out rockery has achieved a natural look.

Periwinkle (Vinca minor), is a common choice for groundcover. It has many attributes: rapid growth, it's evergreen, tolerates sun or shade and has lavender/blue flowers in spring.

annual bocce tournament on, then you're out of luck. Some groundcover varieties can tolerate light foot traffic, but this will have to be infrequent.

Part of the problem with growing a lawn, or even groundcovers, in a shady spot is that because it's shady, it also stays moist for longer periods of time. When growing a lawn or groundcover in shady spots, its best to prepare the area so that there is a gentle slope, allowing excess water to drain away to prevent pooling. And, most importantly, ensure that the soil composition has a high percentage (about 50 percent) of sand for drainage purposes. Roots of any plant need to breathe, but they can't do so when soil is continually moist or wet.

Check out the lawn-alternative plant section on page 183.

Planting &
Transplanting

Planting & Transplanting

M ove it a little to the right…now back a little, now a little to the left…okay…just a little forward, and I think we've got it!

There's a lot more to planting a tree, shrub or even vegetables than just shovelling out a hole and lowering the plant into it. Save yourself some effort, and never dig a planting hole before you know exactly where you want your plant placed. First, set the plant on the spot you think you want it to go, and stand back to have a good look. We definitely don't want to do any more work than is necessary.

Taking extra care, and following some simple steps, can make the difference between short- and long-term success.

"Short-term success" is the plant simply surviving, whereas "long-term success" means a healthy tree or shrub performing exactly as it is supposed to, empowered by the healthy root system that will result from adequate growing conditions.

I often say, "Invest in the hole." A little extra effort devoted to digging an appropriate-sized hole, with the addition of a good selection of soil amendments, can make the difference between life and death, or success and failure.

And there's a lot more to it than just that, so I've tried to give you a plant's perspective on what it requires for the best start possible. Read on to learn more!

Previous page: Always dig and turn the soil in garden beds as deep as possible, as loosened earth will allow crops to grow a deep root system.

PLANTING A POTTED TREE OR SHRUB?

When planting a potted tree or shrub, prepare a hole at least twice the size of the container that it came in—and even bigger is better. Loosening the existing earth and adding in a mix of soil amenders—such as manure, compost, soil and bone meal (see page 192)—will make it easy for your new yard resident to adapt to its adopted surroundings.

TRANSPLANTING AN EXISTING MATURE TREE OR SHRUB?

When transplanting a mature tree or shrub, I recommend you dig it out with as big a rootball as is manageable. The good news is that it is not necessary to dig its new hole too much larger than the size of the root structure remaining on the plant, as the root system is already mature.

It's the end of May and I am still planning on doing some landscaping. When is the latest I can get away with doing this?

A. First of all, good for you! Improving your landscape and getting your yard in shape is important for many reasons, not least that a nicely landscaped yard—compared to a very basic or poorly kept one—can provide a significant increase in the resale value of a home. That can add up to some serious coin, and a pretty good return on investment, considering the majority of the upgrades will come from working out there yourself, or using pizza and beer to coerce family and friends to help.

Planting new additions

There are better times of the year to plant and transplant trees and shrubs than the end of May. Usually February through April—with this period's cooler temperatures and moister conditions—is the best time to landscape. Plants are actively preparing to grow during the spring, which means they'll

In the foreground is the most common hardy geranium, 'Johnson's Blue', zone 4, and behind is a gorgeous pink peony (Paeonia lactiflora cultivar).

Early spring or fall are the optimum seasons to shuffle shrubs around in your yard.

be rooting out and establishing themselves for their first summer and winter in their new location. Taking advantage of those early months in spring is the best way to enable a plant to establish itself, with the lowest risk of failure from the stress of summer heat or a harsh winter.

Fall is another good time to plant trees, shrubs, bulbs and other landscaping plants. Spring holds the title as the winner, but fall is not too hot; light levels are still adequate, moisture is usually frequent and, most importantly, the soil remains warm from the summer months, compliments of Mother

190

Nature. Warm soil specifically encourages root growth that is going to help a plant establish itself relatively quickly. A strong and healthy root system usually means a resilient plant capable of withstanding adversities, such as cold winters, extreme heat and damaging insect infestations.

Having said that, any time you can dig into the ground—that is, when the soil isn't frozen—is actually a fine time to plant. Certainly, any plant you have that needs planting would rather be in the ground than wrapped in burlap, or squeezed into a plastic pot, no matter what time of year it may be.

Planting something in the summer heat does require a little more effort on your part. Obviously, you'll need to ensure the plant has enough moisture to get it growing. However, holding a hose in one hand and a beverage in the other while you get your watering done doesn't sound *too* taxing, now does it?

Moving established plants

A word of caution! When you upgrade your landscape, there is often a need to "shuffle." I'm not referring to the reluctant, shuffling walk of your partner or the rest of your family as you rally them into helping you…I'm speaking of the need to move or remove plants. Plants often mature to a point where they have outgrown their original location. Sometimes it's only a matter of moving a plant over a few feet to prevent it from blocking a window, but this can often start a domino effect. Moving one plant over a few feet places it too close to another plant, so you move that one forward or back, which then affects another plant, and so on…Try to visualize the effect that moving one plant can have on the entire garden bed. Sometimes removing a plant completely might be more appropriate than trying to fit it in.

Moving established outdoor plants is a different situation than introducing new ones from controlled conditions, such as a potted tree from a nursery. Transplanting established plants should be done when those plants are dormant, or just coming out of dormancy. The best time to do your garden shuffle is February through April. If necessary, it can also be done in the fall, but the window of opportunity is small—only late October through November. And plants that are marginally zone appropriate to your area should not be transplanted outside of February through April. So if you're a zone 6 and the plant you want to transplant is a zone 6—meaning it can tolerate the cold of zone 6 but no colder—wait until spring to transplant.

TRANSPLANTING TIPS

Q. *I know that I'm supposed to use a fertilizer when planting shrubs and perennials—which one is best?*

A. Bone meal has been used for decades as a transplanting fertilizer for a few reasons. First, it is all-natural, composed solely of pulverized animal bones, so there is no risk of it burning the plant's roots, like other more manufactured products. Bone meal is also quite high in phosphorus, which stimulates root growth and is important for getting a plant to quickly adapt to its new location. In fact, although phosphorus is important for plants in general, it's specifically needed by newly planted trees, shrubs and perennials. This

After firming down the soil around this dwarf Alberta spruce, water thoroughly. Irrigate freshly planted shrubs regularly to prevent dehydration.

is because a plant's immediate instinct after being transplanted is to force root growth to secure its spot and seek out moisture and nutrients.

Bone meal is normally found in a granular or powder form and sprinkled around the roots of a plant when it is placed in the planting hole, prior to backfilling any soil.

For anything newly planted, the faster it can send out new roots, particularly hair roots, the more readily it will adjust to its new home and the less likely it will be to suffer from environmental stress.

That said, bone meal is slow acting, as it does take some time to break down in the soil and for the nutrition to be made available to the plant. A more recently introduced liquid transplanting fertilizer is touted as being better than bone meal. However, it is not as gentle and organic, so using as directed on the label is critical to ensure it doesn't burn the roots of your plant.

Transplanting liquid contains a similar amount of phosphorus to bone meal, as well as some nitrogen and potash, but it is the liquid format that makes nutrition instantly available to the plant, which will lead to quicker stimulation of root growth. And it also contains an indole butyric acid, a rooting hormone that plants naturally manufacture themselves in the spring months. This rooting hormone, in my opinion, places the liquid transplant fertilizer a notch above bone meal, as it will enable the plant to establish itself more quickly and prevent any threat of transplant shock.

Not sure which way to go? Then simply use both, for the best of both worlds.

When planting a shrub with a burlap sack around the roots, should I remove the sack?

A. When commercial growers dig trees and shrubs, the "ball" or root system is immediately wrapped in a burlap sack to hold all of the roots and soil together. In the industry, this is referred to as "balled and burlapped." The sack is porous so that the roots can readily receive moisture but are not left sitting in overflow that can hinder their growth.

The burlap will begin to rot very quickly once placed in the ground and covered with soil, posing no hindrance to the growing roots. So it's best to leave the sack on the roots so that they are not disturbed. Keeping the roots solid, secure and intact is important in preventing transplant shock, which can mean death to the plant.

To hold the burlap in place, the grower will typically bunch it up around the trunk just above the soil line and tie it firmly with string (usually jute). In time, this could become an issue for the plant, as the string is slow to deteriorate and may girdle the trunk as it tries to grow. So it's best to cut the string—but not before you set the plant in the hole (see below), placed at a depth where the soil level within the burlap sack exactly meets the level of the ground you are planting in.

It's extremely important to dig to the right depth—not too high, and not too low. Too high and roots will be exposed to sun and heat and will dry out through summer—which could damage or even kill the plant. Too low and soil will likely cover a portion of the plant's trunk—which will also threaten its long-term health.

Once the plant is positioned at the appropriate depth, adjust it so that it's upright and straight. I usually press the ball firmly into the hole to ensure everything is held in place and then half backfill to make things more secure.

At this point, cut the string around the top of the sack and fold the sack back so that the soil at the top of the rootball is exposed. This would also be a great time to add your bone meal and/or transplanting liquid (see page 193).

Now backfill with soil so that the folded-back portion of the sack is covered and firmly packed in. Most people are too gentle when it comes to the "firmly" part of packing the soil around the plant. Stamp it in hard with the heel of your boot, as you're trying to give the plant additional support to hold it steady.

Q. *Can I successfully separate and transplant mature cedars that have grown tightly together in a hedge?*

A. Unfortunately, you're not going to be able to separate these trees. As cedars have a very fibrous and matted root system, the roots of your hedge will be so intertwined from tree to tree that they would be near impossible to separate. And cutting those roots to the extent that would be required would undoubtedly kill them.

The other obstacle would be trying to piece the large and very heavy specimens back together so that the barren sides don't show. So in the unlikely event that your trees did survive a transplanting, the resulting effect would probably be unattractive, as any part of the hedging that has had limited light for a period of six months or longer will be brownish and unlikely to ever regenerate growth (see page 130).

Cedars grow quite fast when they're young, then more slowly as they

Separating an established cedar hedge is nearly impossible. Top it, shear it or start over with young cedars.

mature. They tend to send out a flush of growth in the spring, go dormant during summer, and then throw out a second flush of growth in the fall. So you can see a substantial increase in their height annually. My advice is to purchase new 4–6-ft. (1.2–1.8-m) plants as soon as possible and start fresh.

This way is cheaper than buying fully mature cedars, and the only drawback is that you will have lost a little height for the three years or so they will need to reach a mature 12 ft. (3.6 m).

We're digging up our backyard to put in a patio. There are two plants there—a wisteria and clematis. Can I dig these up and transplant them into large pots so that they can stay where they are but not in the ground? What size of pots do you recommend?

Q.

A. It is possible to transplant older wisteria and clematis into containers. Timing is important, with March being the ultimate month to transplant these with success. Since March is a moist, cool time of year, the plant will be less stressed by the move and less likely to suffer transplant shock.

If possible, always move an extracted plant to its new location as soon as you can. Prepare the hole or container using a combination of fresh earth, compost, manure and peat moss or coir. Add bone meal around the roots, or use a high-phosphate transplanting fertilizer (see page 193). This care at the transplanting stage will not only allow new roots to grow quickly and easily

Left: This clematis variety, 'The President', is more than 100 years old and remains very popular today. It grows 8–12 ft. (2.5–3.6 m) and blooms from June to September.

Right: Clematis 'Pink Champagne', zone 4, is an early, large-flowering vine with blooms 5–8 in. (13–20 cm) wide.

into the new location but will also ensure your plants perform much better long term, since they'll be growing in a good mix of assorted mediums.

When choosing the container, think "bigger is better." Vines, in this case, have a massive amount of leaf mass, and during hot periods, those leaves lose a lot of moisture through transpiration (sweating, so to speak)—and all that moisture needs to be replaced. If your container is too small, it will dry out quickly and this will cause damage to the vines, also making them more vulnerable to pests and fungus. Clematis are very susceptable to bacterial diseases and blights. Also, clematis do not like their roots getting too warm, and this is more likely to happen in a pot than in the ground and particularly in a smaller pot.

I suggest 24 × 24 in. (60 × 60 cm) as a minimum size for a container to house your vines, which should provide enough growing space for a large, healthy root system. This will allow plants to perform just as well as if they were in the ground.

Dry spells are your biggest concern, so make sure there is no chance that the soil could become dehydrated.

Often we grow vines against a wall and periodically under an overhang. This could create a problem, as without regular rainfall to water the container, you will be responsible for irrigating 12 months a year. Even in the dead of winter, you need to ensure that the container doesn't go excessively dry.

Q.

I have a red Japanese maple tree, approximately 7 ft. (2 m) high by 5 ft. (1.5 m) wide, which needs to be moved this spring. Could you give me instructions on how to give it a good pruning now so that it has half a chance of surviving?

A. It's a good idea to prune back almost every plant in advance of transplanting, preferably between two and six months prior to the move. It makes the specimen less bulky and, therefore, easier to handle. It will also take away some of the leaf mass, which means the root structure will have less to support while the plant recuperates from the move. Much of a root system is either removed or damaged during transplanting, so it will be easier for the reduced root system to support the lessened upper portion.

Removing a third of the tree would be acceptable, but sometimes even more trimming is better. You may want to accomplish this by pruning some of the central branches to thin the foliage, rather than just the finer branches on the perimeter. Eliminating only perimeter branches may not be enough to reduce the tree by a third. Removing some of the central branches will also open the inside of the tree and allow you to redirect growth and shape as you think best.

A light root pruning would also be beneficial. Based on the size of your tree, insert a sharp spade about 40 in. (1 m) from the trunk, digging as deep into the earth as possible and making a complete circumference of the tree. A root pruning eliminates some roots and reduces the size of the rootball but also encourages the plant to force out an abundance of new root growth within that smaller root framework. Pruning the roots while leaving the plant in place, will make it less likely to suffer any negative repercussion. Then when you dig out the more condensed root structure, removal will be easier and there will be less disturbance to root structure.

Take as much of the root system as you can with the tree, and ensure you plant the tree at the same depth it was previously placed at. Finally, keep the roots moist after the tree has been moved, and use a transplanting liquid fertilizer containing an indole butyric acid (see page 193) to help prevent transplant shock.

All Japanese maples are popular, but red-leafed varieties are more sought after than green leafed. Acer palmatum 'Bloodgood' is the top-selling variety.

Pruning

Just Ask *Wim!*

Pruning is one of the most difficult topics to discuss, because there are so many variables in the decision-making process. How, when and where should you prune? These are just some of the many questions out there...

I always like to comfort gardeners new to pruning with the fact that if you asked 10 experts to prune a similar tree, each one would prune it differently—and all of them would be correct. Yes, there are some essential "how-tos" of pruning, but there are also many varying methods. The best advice I can give you is to simply learn the basics—and prune. Prune as necessary, and watch closely—as identifying what happens to a plant and how it responds to a pruning is one of the greatest teaching tools that the garden can offer.

I do most of my pruning in June. This often baffles people, because so many plants are in full-growth mode. However, there are very few months that go by when I don't prune *something* in my yard. So although pruning is likely one of the more intimidating gardening tasks, I hope I will give you a little insight and enough confidence to just get out there and do it!

Opposite: Loppers are essential for pruning shrubs and trees. Invest in a good-quality pair and they should last you for years.
Below: A bow saw will cut wood in any direction and branches up to 6 in. (15 cm) in diameter. Always remove major limbs as close to the tree's trunk as possible.

PRUNING PLANNER

When should plants be pruned? it's easy to see why people get confused. So many plants, and so many variables. Below is a guideline that you can use as a rule of thumb to determine when to prune the many different categories of plants in your yard. Keep in mind that there are always exceptions.

X = recommended pruning time   O = optional or secondary pruning time

	After blooming	Winter	Summer	Spring	Other	Example
Deciduous non-blooming trees		X	O			Maple Oak
Deciduous blooming trees	X		O			Flowering cherry Magnolia
Deciduous shrubs with berries				X		Calicarpa
Flowering shrubs that bloom on current year's growth		X				Summer-blooming Spirea Late viburnum
Flowering shrubs that bloom on previous year's growth	X					Forsythia Quince
Deciduous non-blooming shrubs		X				Euonymus Alatus
Fruit trees		X	O			Apple Plum
Fruit bushes		X				Blueberry Gooseberry
Evergreen shrubs				O	Late summer	Juniper Pine
Evergreen coniferous hedges				O	Late summer	Cedar Yew
Broadleaf blooming evergreens	X					Rhododendron Kalmia
Broadleaf non-blooming evergreens			O	X		Laurel Acuba

PRUNING BLUEBERRIES

How and when should I prune my blueberries to maximize the production of fruit?

Q.

A. Pruning blueberries annually is essential to maintain their size and shape and, more importantly, to ensure both large and abundant fruit.

The most common error made by the owners of blueberry bushes is keeping too much of their plants intact. Young blueberries should be limited to four main canes from the base root crown, and these are preferably kept in an open, vase-like shape. This open spreading allows for greater light and better airflow, enhancing berry ripening and helping to prevent fungal-disease issues.

Pruning should be completed by the end of January. Many people prune the blueberry in December to take advantage of the colourful stems, displaying them in flower arrangements or poking them into outdoor planters along with added greenery.

A blueberry bush grows canes that then produce branches and side shoots. The fruit is formed on the tips of the side shoots, which were new the previous year, and so the fruit is produced on year-old wood. This may be a bit difficult to picture, but it is a lot more evident with the plant in front of you.

To prune, start by removing all dead or broken canes or stems. Once the plant reaches five years of age, you should also remove the two oldest canes each year—and, believe me, they are easily identifiable, as they will truly look old, with a darkened, grey-brown appearance and possibly crusty lichen and mossy growth covering the stem.

I also always ensure that I eliminate any growth over 5 ft. (1.5 m), as excessive height can both overburden the plant and weigh down branches. Furthermore, it is very difficult to harvest any crop from bushes that become too tall.

Blueberries (Vaccinium) are one of the few fruits native to North America.

WISTERIA WISDOM

Q. *How and when do I prune my wisteria so that I don't lose the blooms?*

A. Pruning a wisteria is not all that difficult—however, timing plays an important role in ensuring you get blooms the following year.

There are many different types of wisteria, but the pruning requirements are similar for all varieties. It is also important to guide your wisteria—not with your wisdom, but with wire, trellis, lattice or some form of wooden framework. This plant grows fast and furiously ("insanely wild" comes to mind) and can also become quite heavy—so thinking ahead to put a support structure in place is, come to think of it, guiding it with your wisdom.

Renovation pruning

Generally, I suggest growing wisteria to the desired height and then topping it, using all of the side shoots to fill the space you would like covered. But if your wisteria is already out of hand, you might want to begin again from square one, using the same plant but giving it a new start with three implements of elimination—your pruners, loppers and a saw.

This major-renovation prune should be done mid winter, because you'll be removing some big limbs, so it's best the plant be dormant. (This is generally true for all plants when it comes to larger limbs.) In winter, there are also no leaves on the vine, so it will be easy to determine where and what to prune. Some discretion will be necessary to determine how far back to cut the vine for this renovation, based on where you find side shoots that you can re-train, but I recommend you aim for somewhere between 3 and 6 ft. (1 and 1.8 m) from ground level.

Come spring, you'll see major growth and dozens of shoots from the remaining portion of the vine. Maintain the strongest 10 to 15 shoots, directing them along your structure or to the preferred height. Remove the excess shoots by ripping them off the trunk. Ripping, rather than pruning, removes the shoots completely, whereas pruning will simply have them growing back. If they're too large to rip off, then saw them off as tight to the trunk as possible.

I should warn you that following a renovation pruning, it could take two to three years for your wisteria to bloom with vigour as it once did.

Chinese wisteria (Wisteria chinenesis), zone 5, has been growing up these supports for many years now. Annual pruning keeps it in good shape.

Annual pruning

Regular biannual prunings are different from a renovation prune. A summer prune will keep the plant somewhat contained, as it can get very unruly. This should be followed by a winter prune, which will be more strategic, as you'll have a better visual of the vine stems because there will be no leaves.

I recommend that you do your summer pruning in July. It's a great job to mark down for the long weekend. Trim down the excessive lateral growth to about four to six sets of leaves. Annual or even more frequent pruning of these laterals to this same level will set them up to harden into spurs that will house blooms.

Your routine winter prune will then consist of simply thinning out, along with removal of any unwanted and overpowering mature, heavy stems. This can be done anytime during the cold season. Again, this is a strategic prune to train and control; you don't want to remove too much, because this would lessen the volume of bloom in spring/summer.

Finally, take note of what happens after you prune—you can learn lots by identifying how a plant—any plant—responds to a trim. Taming the dragon really is possible!

PRUNING ROSES

I enjoyed my first two rose bushes this year—a grandiflora and a hybrid tea. When is the best time to prune them, and how much should I remove?

A. The first dormant pruning of your rose bushes should take place in late October in colder regions and during November in more moderate climates. I say "dormant," even though there may still be a few leaves remaining on the plants. During these times, you can take off about a third of the plant. Branches that might trap snow, and possibly break off, should be removed. Also, get rid of any remaining leaves, as well as old buds or blossoms, as they can harbour insects or diseases that would re-infect your plants the following season.

March is the best time to do your final dormant pruning for the big blooming season ahead. Rose bushes are generally not pruned back hard enough. When you're finished, the stems should be, on average, 12 in. (30 cm) for hybrid teas and 18 in. (45 cm) for floribunda and grandiflora varieties. These stems should all be solid, sturdy wood capable of supporting the weight of an abundance of foliage and blossoms.

This beautiful red hybrid tea rose will reward you with ample blooms if you prune it hard each March. Pruning rejuvenates and invigorates roses.

AZALEA MAINTENANCE

I have azaleas in my garden, and they have done very well. I like that they are green year round. How far do I cut them back for winter?

A. For the most part, you do not need to prune azaleas, as these plants are relatively self-maintaining. However, there are times when it is best to keep them in check, or prune to maintain fullness.

Never prune azaleas in fall or winter. It won't damage the plant, but you'll be pruning off all the blossoms for the following spring. Instead, shortly after it completes its blooming cycle in the spring, shear 2–4 in. (5–10 cm) off the top and sides—sort of like giving it a bit of a brush cut.

The new growth from that point on should set flower buds for the following year. Also consider applying a light mulch of coir or peat moss annually in spring around the base of each plant.

Above: *Azalea 'Hino Crimson', zone 6, is a large-growing broadleaf evergreen that is a hardy, low-growing and profuse bloomer.*

Q. *Do I need to cut back the lovely rhododendron in my garden? If so, how much?*

Top right: *Use this violet azalea as an accent plant, in borders or for foundation planting. March and April are the best months to find it at garden centres.*

A. The rhododendron family is huge, with some warm-climate varieties and others just fine with the cold but temperate northern winters. There are also varieties that grow to only 1 ft. (30 cm), whereas others can dwarf a small house. Similar traits and care requirements generally apply to all sizes.

First, the timing is important to ensure you don't prune off the buds that will offer blooms the following spring. The ultimate time to prune a rhodo is right after it has finished flowering. Pruning times will vary because of the varying bloom times of the rhododendron family—starting in March, with some that don't bloom until May or even June.

You don't have to prune rhodos annually; however, removing the spent flower stems keeps them looking tidy. Grasp the spent flower stem at its base and bend it until it snaps off the plant. Usually, it will break off right above new growth buds.

Don't go more than three or, maximum, four springs without pruning, as this regenerates new growth and keeps the plant full, compact and even. Be aware that rhodos have stems that harden, meaning they age to a rough bark-type consistency. As they do not sprout new growth easily from hardened stems, regular pruning of your rhodos will spare you the risk of cutting into this older growth. Nevertheless, from time to time, a rhodo may require removal of larger limbs for varying reasons. Don't be afraid to remove limbs as necessary to keep the plant in good form. This can be done at any time of the year, and removal should be tight to the adjoining limb.

The huge blossoms of the rhododendron family are stunning and available in a wide variety of colours, but select wisely because many varieties won't tolerate cold climates.

ENCOURAGING HYDRANGEA TO FLOWER

I have two hydrangea plants that seem to have stopped flowering. Am I pruning them at the wrong time? They are both facing south and the green leaves are very plentiful.

A. Hydrangeas are an interesting family in that there is so much diversity within the species. The first thing you'll need to know is the variety or category of hydrangea that you have. Care and maintenance will vary depending on this, particularly when it comes to pruning. Having a hydrangea appropriate for your zone is also important. A variety that is outside of its usual zone tolerances may experience much dieback from the cold if unprotected, and although it will regrow from the crown, it is unlikely to blossom that season.

A hydrangea blossom might take a little annual maintenance to keep it rich blue.

All hydrangeas prefer a moderately bright location, ideally with morning sun and afternoon shade. Hydrangeas have so much leaf mass that when exposed to the hot afternoon sun they can transpire and exhaust themselves. That is also one of the reasons they prefer growing in a cool, moist soil, and an annual spring mulching will assist in soil-moisture retention.

Pruning plays an important role in flower production. Pruning incorrectly or at the wrong time of year can prevent blooming. The two most popular categories of hydrangea are *Hydrangea macrophylla* (the mophead varieties—usually pink or blue—with the big round flower head) and *H. paniculata* (PG), with its cone-shaped flower heads.

The macrophylla family blooms off old wood (stems that have been on the plant since the summer before the current season). I suggest removing stems with the old blossoms from that season, cutting them down to approximately 6 in. (15 cm) from the crown of the plant. Leave stems that have no blossoms unpruned, as they carry the flower buds for the following year.

The paniculata (PG) family require a much easier and less complicated pruning task. Come late fall, pruning should be harsh. I take mine down to approximately the size of a basketball. This can vary slightly depending on the variety. This family blooms on new growth from the current season, and so nearly all the new growth from a sturdy base of stems will produce a flower bud.

One last thing: too much shade, which can often evolve in a garden over time as trees and shrubs mature, can reduce flowering to such an extent that hydrangeas in full shade will not usually bloom.

MAPLE

My maple is getting too large. How, where and when should I prune it?

Q.

A. This is a great question, because there are so many varieties of maple, numbering in the hundreds, and as a whole they're extremely popular—including those that grow only a couple of feet tall to others that reach nearly a couple of hundred feet.

I'll speak generally about how one should prune a maple, because it is such a broad family. First, you should be aware that by pruning your maple, you will encourage the growth of a much fuller tree. This can be either good or bad—a bushier maple might be perfect for your landscape, but then again it might not be, as a fuller tree takes up a lot more space.

In my front yard, I have a green vine maple. It is not an excessively large-growing variety and, thanks to my periodic pruning, is only about 20 ft. (6 m) tall. My pruning efforts are not a scheduled program by any means. Although many gardening books provide very specific times to prune a maple, I have probably pruned it at least once every month over its 16 years of growing in my yard. My most diligent efforts involve slight thinning or lighter trimming of some of the longer seasonal growth during the summer months, with a more in-depth and heavy pruning during the winter months, but some years I do this and other years I don't bother at all. So pruning a maple can be quite flexible and much of the "when" is based on how the tree is looking, as well as the size, height and width you desire.

Getting your maple down to size

If your maple is getting too large, then you'll need to give it a hard winter pruning. This is different from summer pruning, as it's much easier to get a good overall sense of the shape on a dormant, leafless tree—or what I like to call the skeleton of the tree. So much of pruning is based on visualizing what the growing results will be afterward, which is why I suggest that people take time to observe what happens to a tree the following season after pruning.

To get your maple down to size, assuming it's a relatively mature tree, you are going to need a saw. Yes…I said "saw." You can do this! It is pretty near impossible to kill a maple from pruning, so your success is basically guaranteed.

Keep in mind that you don't want to prune to the exact size you want your tree to grow to, because the tree is going to put on an abundance of growth from just below where you pruned. So you might want to consider taking it down by up to half the size it is now. Symmetry is the order of the day here—prune so that when you stand back and look at the tree, you will not feel like there are any lopsided branches and that the length of a branch

Maple trees are a glorious garden accent, with their many diverse and unique characteristics over hundreds of varieties. But their rich fall colours really make them special.

on one side of the tree is relatively similar to a corresponding branch on the other. It can never be perfect, but a sense of balance is what you're looking to create.

Preferably, prune just above a node (a bump in a branch, where side branches previously grew). If you're apprehensive about how much to prune, prune a branch to a lesser extent to start, and then go back to prune further if it looks like more needs to be removed to achieve balance. It's always easier to give a second prune, as opposed to pruning too hard the first time.

LILACS

When do I prune a lilac hedge?

Q.

A. Wow…a lilac hedge. Now that must be beautiful in bloom…but it will also be a big job to prune.

You can prune a lilac at any stage, but the best time is right after it blooms. I recommend that you remove no more than a third of each branch. I also like to remove sucker growth from the ground, so that the bush doesn't get excessively bushy and unmanageable. Lilacs also tend to have a fair amount of dieback, so it's important to remove any deadwood, or branches without leaves.

Overall, you should work your lilac so that it's continually rejuvenating itself. Branches will age to the extent that they produce fewer flowers, and removing some of the older, larger branch structure will make room for younger, more productive sucker growth from the base of the tree. With ongoing maintenance and strategic pruning, you can also keep your lilac down to a manageable 15 ft. (4.5 m) or so.

Major rejuvenation pruning

If your lilac has not been pruned for quite some time, then you might need a major rejuvenation pruning, which would dramatically reduce the number of blooms the following spring but would also get the plant down to a manageable size.

Usually performed after blooming, a rejuvenation prune takes half of the older, taller stems down to ground level and reduces the remaining half by a third in height. Let's call this second batch the "B stems." If there are a lot of new recovery shoots from the ground the following season, you might now want to take down to ground level those older "B stems" that avoided the wrath of your pruners the previous year. If the harsh pruning did not result

Lilacs are beautiful in bloom, particularly as the scent fills the yard.

in abundant new shoots the following spring, you may want to postpone the pruning of "B stems" until the next spring after blooming.

Partial rejuvenation pruning

If you don't want to sacrifice too many blooms, though, you can take a partial approach to rejuvenation pruning. You might only want to reduce some of the branches by half to three-quarters, to thin the bush overall but leave some of the other branches. By strategically removing branches throughout the plant over two or three years, you can get the plant down in size yet still allow for a healthy amount of bloom the following spring.

Whichever method you choose, the most important rule is not to prune after the summer, as this would remove the flower buds for the following spring.

Garden Pests
& Problems

I don't think I've ever heard anyone say anything negative about gardening—other than, perhaps, about the exertion required. And even this lament is generally tongue in cheek, because every bit of effort is so amply rewarded and, in the scheme of things, not really that onerous.

However, there is one little subcategory within gardening that does raise some genuine angst…and that is pesticides—even the word sounds nasty!

But do you know that salt, dish soap and even vinegar are all pesticides? So, evidently, we can't let ourselves get hung up on a word. You might also know that some organic pesticides are actually more toxic than conventional options. That said, the organic choices generally are much safer and should be our first line of defence. I go to great lengths to recommend organic options over chemical methods of pest control, and within this chapter, you'll even find some of my homemade recipes to control pesky critters.

Without a doubt, there are many bad bugs, weeds, fungal diseases and other pests that need to be controlled throughout our yard and within our home, and the trick is to always manage them within the safest methods possible. When you have a pest issue, investigate all the control options, choosing the most responsible strategy—because that is what is best for you, your plants and the environment long term.

Prevention, however, is still the top method of eliminating or at least dramatically minimizing problems. We've all heard "an apple a day keeps the doctor away." But what about the apple tree? What is the apple's preventative medicine? Well, there are many steps that can be taken to prevent pests and disease for an apple tree, a strawberry plant in a container, a lawn, a cedar hedge or a houseplant. Proper pruning, cleaning up of debris at the end of the season, regular visual checks, removal of any in-season diseased leaves, limited sprinkling (with an emphasis on watering early in the day), optimal nourishment, attracting beneficial insects to your outdoor space…these are among the many good gardening habits that can help to prevent problems before they even start.

It is particularly important to have a bee lure, such as the perennial bee balm, if you have fruiting trees and bushes in your yard. The bees will check out their flowers and do a little pollinating at the same time.

Just Ask *Wim!*

DORMANT OIL

Each spring and summer, I see insect infestations on my fruit trees. I hear that dormant oil spraying is the best way to prevent insect and fungal infestations—what is dormant oil spraying, and exactly when do I do this?

Q.

A. You're right. Dormant oil spraying of fruit trees (and roses) will smother overwintering adult insects and their eggs before they can get going in the spring. Sprayed during the dormant season, when insects are inactive and before the buds have opened on your trees, horticultural oil is an effective and ecological way to control mites, scale, mealy bugs, codling moth, red spider, whiteflies, aphids, leaf rollers and other problems. The addition of lime sulphur to most dormant-oil kits makes it an effective fungicide too.

Spraying three times over the winter, while your tree or rose bush is dormant and before any buds have begun to open, will provide a huge advantage in your upcoming growing season. Space your applications three to four weeks apart and be sure to spray on a dry day that is above freezing and not windy (with no rain expected for three days).

Protect yourself from the spray by wearing a hat, long sleeves, gloves and eye goggles. Prior to spraying, cover surrounding shrubs and perennials with a tarp to prevent foliage damage. Drench the trunk and branches with the oil, being careful that it doesn't drip on you while you work. Leave the protective tarp in place until the dripping has subsided and oil has dried.

PLANT PESTS

I have spider mite on my indoor umbrella tree, along with aphids on my outdoor rose bush. Is there one organic insecticide that will control both problems?

Q.

A. Plant pests both inside and out can be extremely frustrating! I have four lively boys, so I'm bugged enough without any additional pest problems. No spray will make my boys behave! There is, however, something I recommend that is both organic and thorough enough for a wide assortment of insect issues, inside and out. The product is Safer's Insecticidal Soap. This is an organic insecticide made from naturally-occurring plant oils and animal fats. The soap penetrates the outer shell of soft-bodied insect pests and causes dehydration and death within hours.

Often, the same insects that attack your outdoor shrubs and flowers also attack your indoor houseplants. Mites, aphids, whiteflies and mealy bugs can be found both in your living room and your flower beds. Fortunately, Safer's Soap is effective on all of these pests! Also worthy of note, it does not harm beneficial insects like the lovely ladybug and leaves no chemical residue.

Safer's Soap is OMRI Listed. This is a certification granted from the Organic Materials Review Institute, a private, non-profit organization that determines whether or not products qualify as organic under the USDA's National Organic Program. Products that are found to comply are listed on the OMRI Brand Name Products List (BNPL). The list is used by organic certifiers, growers, manufacturers and suppliers to confirm that a product is organic according to USDA rules.

Like most organic insecticides, Safer's Soap does not have a long lifespan on a plant. These products degenerate quickly in sunlight and simply wash off with rainfall or sprinkling. This is why regular sprayings every 7–14 days are necessary to ensure complete eradication of a given insect. Safer's products (they also have a fungicide product) are available from your local garden centre, and should always be used as directed on the label.

If you do decide to spray your indoor plants, place them on newspaper to catch the dripping, or if the weather is appropriate, take outdoors and spray them over your lawn area. Also, when spraying outdoors, plan to apply any sprays early morning or evening rather than during the heat of the day. If sprays are applied in direct sunlight you can lose up to half of the spray due to rapid evaporation and also run the risk of burning the foliage. Lastly, never spray a dry plant with any insecticide—make sure the plant is well hydrated before beginning.

Insects can often blend in and go unnoticed while they suck the life out of plants. Get up close and personal with your plants regularly, as the best time to control a problem is early on, before too much damage is done.

216

APHIDS ON FLOWERS

I've had terrible luck with aphids on my lupines and roses and everything else nearby. And in this area, the soil appears puffed up, and I see ants. What can I do to control this situation?

Q.

A. The best way to control aphids is to spot-treat when you notice them. If numbers are small, you might first want to try to rinse them off with a stiff spray of water from the hose. Otherwise, you can get quick control with a pyrethrum spray (derived from the chrysanthemum flower), which can be used on almost every plant and crop to instantly kill aphids on contact.

If you notice ants on a plant, this is frequently a signal that there are aphids on it, too (see page 218). You'll often be surprised by what you see when you get up close and personal with your plants. Looking at your trees, shrubs, flowers and vegetables from a distance may not give you any indication of whether they are infested. Periodically jiggling each plant while holding a piece of white paper beneath its leaves can also help to identify problems, as many insects shake off easily and viewing them on a light background makes them stand out. Getting control of an insect infestation early will allow you to deal with the issue before too much damage is done.

An aphid infestation can look daunting as they cling to plants by the thousands. You can control the problem easily by hand, with a stiff spray of water or with one of the many natural organic insecticides on the market. Or release ladybugs and watch them devour the aphids.

Right: A hungry ladybug can help resolve an aphid infestation.

LADYBUG, LADYBUG

In spring, garden centres sell ladybugs (a few hundred per package), and these hungry, beneficial insects will search out and feast on most species of aphids.

CARROT TOPS

Let a small patch of carrots go to flower in your vegetable garden. Their blossoms are sweetly fragrant and attract beneficial insects to your garden and, more particularly, to your organic vegetable garden.

Right: An ant harvesting honeydew excreted by aphids to take it back to the ant nest for distribution.

ANTS IN YOUR PLANTS

Ants are not necessarily a problem unless they start invading your patio or are marching right into your home. People often believe ants are chomping on their plants, but these insects feed on the excretion (honeydew) of the aphids, so they will follow them for this food source. In fact, ants will redirect aphids or even carry them to new plants to start additional colonies where they can collect more honeydew for their nearby nest.

Ants do not usually damage plants and really are more of a pest than a problem. If needed, you can control ants by using bait containing the natural killing ingredient borax.

ATTRACTING THE GOOD GUYS

Bug wars are taking place in our gardens every day, and often we don't even know it. Good against evil. We refer to the good guys—lacewings, syrphid (or hover) flies, ladybugs and more—as beneficial insects, and these helpers eat up bad guys, such as the aphids that are harming our plants. We can attract the good guys by including specific plants in our garden. This is the ultimate way to organically control insect pests in the garden! Consider adding one or more of these plants to attract beneficial insects to your yard:

Annual flowers that attract beneficial insects

- **Alyssum (*Lobularia maritima*)**
- **Calendula, or pot marigold (*Calendula officinalis*)**
- **Cornflower (*Centaurea* sp.)**
- **Cosmos (*Cosmos bipinnatus*)**
- **Love in a mist (*Nigella damascena*)**
- **Marigold, or tagetes (*Tagetes* sp.)**
- **Zinnia (*Zinnia elegans*)**

Herbs that attract beneficial insects

- **Anise hyssop (*Agastache foeniculum*)**
- **Basil (*Ocimum basilicum*)**
- **Bronze fennel (*Foeniculum vulgare* 'Purpureum')**
- **Cilantro/coriander (*Coriandrum sativum*)**
- **Chive (*Allium schoenoprasum*)**
- **Dill (*Anethum graveolens*)**
- **Garlic chive (*Allium tuberosum*)**
- **Lavender (*Lavandula angustifolia*)**
- **Lemon balm (*Melissa officinalis*)**
- **Mint (*Mentha spicata*)**
- **Parsley (*Petroselinum crispum*)**

Perennials that attract beneficial insects

- **Basket of gold (*Alyssum saxatilis*)**
- **Bee balm (*Monarda didyma*)**
- **Purple coneflower (*Echinacea purpurea*)**
- **Penstemon (*Penstemon strictus*)**
- **Viola (*Viola*)**
- **Yarrow (*Achillea* sp.)**

Top: *Calendula flowers in a field.*
Middle: *The cosmos annual attracts butterflies.*

Bottom: *Don't swat this guy. Lacewings, like ladybugs, help control insect pests in the garden.*

SLUG AND SNAIL CONTROL

Q. *What is the best way to control slugs? I've tried the beer-in-the-sunken-container trick without much success, and I don't really want sunken containers all over my yard.*

A. Controlling slugs by feeding them beer seems be a waste of a good beverage. Well, unless you use a light beer.

The old beer trick does work; however, having little plastic containers all over your yard can look unattractive. You also need to empty them regularly, and if you live in a rainy part of the country, you'll simply have water-filled containers that won't do anything to control your slug issue.

In dry weather, however, the beer-filled sunken container works as a lure and a "drunk tank." Simply sink a 4-in. (10-cm) cottage-cheese container, or something similar, completely into the ground. Fill with approximately 3 in. (7.5 cm) of beer, and your trap is set.

Slugs are attracted to the yeast in the beer and slither over the side of the container to indulge. I'm not sure if they fall into the beer-filled vat because they drink to complete inebriation or if they tipple until they're top heavy, then topple in. Either way, they drown both themselves and their sorrows in

Snails hide in nooks and crannies, but their presence will be evident by the notched edges of leaves from their feeding throughout the night.

the beer. This method is not the most pleasant way to control slugs in your yard, but it does work.

Another option is the all-natural slug baits available from your local garden centre. Ensure that you pick the environmentally friendly brand that won't harm pets, children or wildlife.

WHITEFLIES

My potted tomato plant has whiteflies—what can I use to get rid of them?

Q.

A. Not only are they a big annoyance, but whiteflies can also do great harm to tomato plants.

Whiteflies sucking nutrients from the leaves can deteriorate a plant to an extent that limits crop size or even kills the plant.

Since this is an edible crop, more than ever, we don't want to use harsh chemicals. But the good news is that there are safe ways to control whiteflies:

1. Yellow sticky-paper traps are a simple and marginally effective means of controlling whiteflies. They are attracted to the yellow colour and get stuck to the adhesive. You could also smear petroleum jelly onto a piece of yellow cardboard for a similar approach.

2. For quicker control, you can use the organic pyrethrum products that will kill on contact. Many people suggest that sprays are not effective, but these sprays do work. The shortcoming of sprays can be that even when the flies are dead, the eggs, laid by the female whitefly on the underside of upper leaves, are continually hatching (every 5 to 10 days), making it seem like control is impossible. For this reason, it's necessary to spray frequently (at least weekly) to completely eradicate the infestation.

3. I highly recommend that you also spray with liquid seaweed fertilizer, particularly on the undersides of the plant's leaves, as this makes those areas undesirable for the whitefly to lay eggs, and of course, seaweed is completely organic and safe (for more on this, see page 240.)

The rich, dark and healthy leaves on this tomato show the difference that feeding with organic fertilizer and compost tea can make. A healthy and bountiful crop should follow.

AILING HOUSEPLANTS

Q. *Why do the leaves of so many of my houseplants turn yellow over the winter months?*

A. The biggest killer, or at least hardship, for houseplants over the winter months is overwatering. Like outdoor plants, our indoor plants go dormant over winter because of very low light levels; therefore, their water requirements also diminish.

Usually, you can cut back your watering by half from November through April. Even then, ensure the soil is relatively dry before you water. And it's always wise to check your plants regularly, because even though all plants require less water, those that haven't been repotted in years and are root-bound might still dry out relatively quickly. My word of advice is that you can do more harm by overwatering than you can by underwatering.

Another reason for yellowing houseplant leaves over winter can be a common home invader called spider mite. This sucking insect digs its fangs

Adding a little life inside your home with houseplants can not only enhance your décor but also help purify the air.

into the plant's leaves to draw out nourishment. It can do this multiple times a day, each time leaving a tiny chlorophyll-depleted white spot. Multiply that by possibly hundreds or even thousands of spider mites and it's easy to see why a plant can quickly begin to look yellowy or lighter in colour.

Spider mite is a pest that enjoys the dry, warm environment of our winter-heated homes, so check the back of the leaves periodically for an extremely small (nearly microscopic), spider look-alike. Another telltale sign that your plants are infested by spider mite is fine webbing in the crotch of some of the leaves. Misting regularly with tepid water will help discourage most houseplant pests.

Q. *A year ago, I used unsterilized potting soil for my indoor plants and ended up with little flies (like fruit flies). Someone suggested I take all the plants out of the soil, hose them off, and then put them into sterilized soil. I did that, but the flies are back. How can I eliminate this problem?*

A. You are likely dealing with fungus gnats—irritating little flies that can be detrimental to your plants because they feed on the roots.

Although short-lived, their reproductive skills are impressive, and that's why it seems like there is an ever-growing population. Fungus gnats search out decaying material and fruit and love the moist soil of houseplants as a place to lay their eggs.

The first step in eliminating these pests is to let the top of the soil of your houseplants go dry. I also recommend that you take a kitchen fork and scuff the top of the soil to offer better aeration, which should change the soil's characteristics and make it a less attractive location for fungus gnats to lay their eggs. These simple steps will make a dramatic difference in controlling this pest. The adult fungus gnat lives for only about seven days, so clearly there needs to be a breeding ground for it to continue to populate your home.

As well, use these tips to eliminate the fungus gnat:

1. Keep fruit and vegetables in the fridge.

2. Spray the top of your houseplants' soil weekly with a mixture made with 2 tsp (10 mL) of dish soap to 4 cups (1 L) of water.

3. You can also mix 2 tsp (10 mL) of bleach to 4 cups (1 L) of water and again spray the soil surface of your houseplants weekly.

4. Or you can purchase an insecticidal soap from your local garden centre and, again, on a weekly basis spray the surface of the soil.

Bottom: *Although often considered a weed because of its invasive nature, it is easily forgiven when we enjoy sweet and juicy blackberries mid summer.*

BOTTLE TRAP

After some experimenting, I've had great success with my plastic water-bottle trap as part of the solution to fungus gnats and fruit flies.

Carefully poke with a pencil point or the tip of a sharp knife 6 small holes around the upper part of an empty water bottle. Next, pour in ½–1 in. (1–2.5 cm) of balsamic vinegar and 1 tsp (5 mL) of dish soap. Replace the cap. Swirl the mixture around in the bottle gently and then watch the insect pests flock to it and make their way through the holes, staying trapped inside the bottle and eventually drowning in the vinegar.

INVASIVE BLACKBERRIES

Q. *The nearby blackberries have started to infiltrate our yard—what should we do?*

A. Blackberries can be an invasive and nasty plant.
First, I would say that the earlier you grab control of your blackberry situation, the better. The longer you wait to deal with any weed infestation— budding in the lawn, spreading in the garden or encroaching on your

Blackberries (Rubus fruticosa), compete with all flora surrounding it for water, light and nutrition. Don't let it get a foot in your yard or it will take a mile!

shrubbery—the more it will root, spread and become more difficult to control.

So, what is the best means of controlling blackberry? Cut it down—you must stop the plant in its tracks, as blackberries can invade like a full-throttle freight train. From there, you can try to pull up some of the roots to reduce the length of this long-term battle. As to who will win; it comes down to who is more persistent—you or the blackberry.

Most importantly, you must not let it leaf out, as all those pieces of root left behind in the soil are going to want to sprout, and once they do, they'll be able to absorb the sun, create their sugars for energy, and away they'll grow. Again, do not let them leaf out! Pulling leaves off and roots out on a daily basis, if need be, is what will be required to win this war!

Rally the troops, arm yourselves (with thorn-resistant garden gloves), and good luck, soldiers.

DIGGING DOGS

Are there any plants I can add to my garden to deter my dog from digging it up?

A. Some dogs require that a yard be barren. I have a friend in a similar situation: he has a Labradoodle who loves to tunnel through the garden—and also seems to think the house is in the way and is trying to remove it one vinyl-siding piece at a time.

A lawn keeps not just kids happy.

Unfortunately, there really isn't a lot you can do to prevent a dog like that from following his instincts. Some dogs can be trained to stay out of certain gardens, but that can sometimes be a large and time-consuming project likely to fail. Maybe it's time to consider a rock garden. But, then again, some dogs like rocks…

One strategy you can try is to replace some of those dog-discarded plants with others of the prickly persuasion. Here are a few dog-gone uncomfortable plants:

POOCH PUT-OFFS

The zones indicated in this book are the minimum hardiness zones per genus. Individual cultivar hardiness zones could vary. Check with your local nursery for clarification.

- **Cotoneaster (*Cotoneaster lacteus*)** – zone 5, grows to 12 ft. (3.6 m), evergreen with red berries

- **Firethorn (*Pyracantha*)** – zone 5, thorns, fast-growing with red or orange berries

- **Holly (*Ilex × meserveae*)** – zone 5, slow-growing to 8 ft. (2.5 m), female has red berries

- **Juniper (*Juniperus × pfitzeriana*)** – zone 4, grows 4–6 ft. (1.2–1.8 m), good for foundation planting

- **Mugo pine (*Pinus mugo*)** – zone 2, extremely hardy and adaptable conifer

Above: *Introduced from Europe in 1779, mugo pine (Pinus mugo) are well suited to Canadian climates. They can be found in eastern Canada as well as Alberta and British Columbia.*
Left: *A healthy firethorn shrub (Pyracantha coccinea) is coaxed to grow along a fence. In the winter, its plump berries will be a favourite of birds.*

- **Oregon grape (*Mahonia nervosa*)** – zone 6, slow-growing shrub with leaves that resemble holly, yellow flowers

- **Shrub rose (*Rosa rugosa*)** – zone 3, very spiny stems, multicoloured blooms, hardy, low maintenance

- **Wintergreen barberry (*Berberis julianae*)** – zone 6, upright evergreen suitable for hedging, small yellow spring flowers, thorns

- **Yucca (*Yucca filamentosa*)** – zone 5, sword-shaped leaves with tall, white bloom spike

LANDSCAPE FABRIC

I like the idea of landscape fabric to keep weeds down, but my friend says they will just grow through it. Is there anything else that will suppress weeds?

Well, a couple of feet of concrete oughta do the trick.

Okay, landscape fabric is meant to control weeds, and it does! The woven black fabric is more than sufficient to suppress weed growth.

There are many different thicknesses/grades that can control weeds, with a warranty from between five to twenty-five years! That's a pretty solid weed-control commitment.

It's not usually because of a problem with the fabric that we see weeds growing through gravel, lava rock or bark mulch (three of the more common materials used on top of landscape fabric to weigh it down and offer a decorative covering). So why are weeds growing through a covered area?

There are two basic reasons why you'll see this relatively uncommon occurrence. The first is that sometimes the gardener neglects to overlay the strips of fabric. Landscape fabric is usually available in 3-ft. (90-cm) strips. Overlapping the strips by 3 in. (7.5 cm) will ensure the weeds are contained.

The second reason is that the mulch material on top of the fabric has decayed to the extent that it has become a growing medium, and weed seeds have blown in and are growing in the mulch. Or enough dust and soil debris has blown in and settled on the rock, and washed down to the top of the fabric, creating a germinating ground for weed seeds. The irony of this is that the rock covering becomes a mulch that ensures the small layer of soil on top of the fabric doesn't dry out—an ideal weed-growing situation.

To prevent weeds from growing on top of the fabric, you must periodically clean out the rock and sweep or blow the fabric every couple of years, or as required. A bark mulch covering is a little more difficult to clean, so simply nipping those seedlings in the bud is often the best means of controlling potential weed infestations. The weeds' roots cannot grow down and through the fabric, so they are easy to pull out. Alternatively, you could use one of the environmentally friendly weed killers or a vinegar solution sprayed directly on the weeds on a sunny day.

MAKE YOUR OWN WEED SPRAY

Sprayed directly onto a weed, this solution will burn all top growth. Do not use it on your lawn or around tender annuals or perennials, as overspray could harm good plants, and the solution could damage roots.

½ cup (125 mL) lemon-juice concentrate

4 cups (1 L) white or cider vinegar

2 Tbsp (30 mL) liquid dishwashing soap

DISCOURAGING MOLES

> *I have a mole, or many moles, leaving piles of dirt around my yard and destroying my lawn and plants. How can I get rid of them?*

Q.

A. Moles make tunnels, often throughout someone's lawn and garden, as a means for finding food. Soil-bound grubs and worms drop into the tunnels, and the moles routinely travel through their network of passageways to seek out this culinary sacrifice. To dig their tunnels, moles push the excess soil up above surface level. This creates those mounds we call molehills.

Many gardeners are inclined to eliminate the molehill with the old "stomp-until- it's-relatively-flat method." Don't do this! First, there is no way that you can stomp hard enough for that mound to become completely level with the surrounding soil, and clomping on the mound does nothing to fill the tunnel. Leaving the tunnels unfilled will only create sinkholes in the lawn as they collapse over time.

The best method to eliminate the mounds, as well as fill the tunnels, is to bring out the hose. Aim the water at the centre of the mound, which will have it finding its way into the tunnel. The soil of the now-muddy mound will follow the water down into the tunnel, eliminating both completely. This

Moles are destructive and not all that cute and cuddly. Gardeners find themselves at odds with this subterranean tyrant, with limited control options.

won't discourage the mole, however, or even deter him. The next day you could see that mound pushed right back up again.

I have heard many mole repellents through the years that simply don't work. Here are just a few that you can dismiss immediately:

- A stick of Juicy Fruit gum down the hole
- A whirligig stuck into a molehill
- Cayenne pepper sprinkled into the hole

And there are other methods that, in my opinion, offer marginal to little success:

- A vibrating mole repeller
- Mole gassers
- Garlic planted around the yard

Traps are the most effective option, and although we don't want to make a mountain out of a molehill, there is no doubt that moles can cause a lot of damage and plant destruction with their voracious tunnelling.

Soil Building, Composting & Feeding Your Plants

Soil Building, Composting & Feeding Your Plants

Every living creature on earth needs nourishment—and plants are no exception.

Some might wonder why we need to fertilize, when plants are capable of creating their own food through photosynthesis. Isn't this enough? This is a great question, and my answer is that it's best to guarantee that our plants have received sufficient nutrition so that they are at optimum health and look their best. Good nourishment ensures the richest leaf colours, an abundance of flowers, and vigorous fruit and vegetable growth for large, bountiful crops. Similar to you and me, plants will be healthier and more resistant to disease and insect infestations when they eat well—and this is particularly important when we garden organically.

It is also important to recognize that most plants are not growing in their usual environment or nutrient-rich soil to begin with. The average home built over the past few decades was constructed in a subdivision where the original nutrition-laden topsoil was scraped off and construction fill was trucked in to preload and elevate the land. The small amount of topsoil later brought in for landscaping purposes is barely enough to grow a lawn on.

Soil is vital for success, and plants growing in rich earth will develop a larger root system and grow much better than they could in hardpan or a heavy, clay-based situation. Healthy soil will also retain fertilizer, as the colloids collect useful elements and hold them for when the plants need them. Mulching and what I call "compost-cycling" are also integral to keeping a landscape lush and crops protected. When we improve our soil, we improve our results.

There are many types of fertilizers, and it can be very confusing and overwhelming to decide on the appropriate one for each plant. There's soluble, liquid, granular, slow release...You could end up with a garage stuffed full of bags and boxes of fertilizer, much of it probably unnecessary.

Whenever possible, using the appropriate fertilizer for a specific plant or crop is better, but you don't need to match everything perfectly. Yes, a nice medium-rare, heavily spiced steak is my preference, but I'm good with a humbler soup, too. Although I do use some specific fertilizers throughout my yard, a generic and organic 6-8-6 in early spring on pretty much every plant is a basic meal that benefits all.

Previous page:
Loosening the earth and mixing deep compost, manure or coir helps vent a heavy soil, which is difficult for young vegetables to root into.

CREATING COMPOST

I would like to start a compost box. Can you tell me what I should or should not put in it and provide some tips for success?

Q.

A. I have been "compost-cycling" for nearly 30 years and highly recommend it for anyone with a yard.

Making compost is one of the easiest and most beneficial things you can do for your garden. Composting is a process that involves piling raw organic matter—such as grass clippings, leaves, kitchen scraps and more—into a compost box. Through decomposition, all of these materials transform into a

Compost should be loose, dark and soil-like. Composting is not only a huge benefit to the garden but also a great way to help our fragile environment.
Jay Shaw photo

rich loamy soil/compost. All you need is a compost box, which you can build yourself or purchase from your local garden centre. Note that a variety of waste materials will assist with the all-important aeration. Mixing green and heavy kitchen waste with dried twigs, branches, leaves or less dense garden waste will offer a good balance that should ensure good air circulation, drainage and heat buildup.

I compost for three reasons:

1. Free soil/compost: compost (the end result of the composting process) is *the* most affordable way to improve your garden's soil composition. Composting allows you to eliminate so much of your kitchen and yard waste, and shortly afterward, you are rewarded with free, rich and nutritious compost for your garden and planters. Adding compost to your planter boxes and pots, as mulch for shallow-rooted plants, or mixing it into your vegetable garden, will improve the health of plants and increase their insect- and disease-resistance—and make them much more likely to provide you with bountiful crops and flowers.

2. Compost tea: liquid fertilizer derived from your compost is a great organic way to feed your plants. Although compost tea is not rich in the major nutritional elements nitrogen, phosphate and potash, it is abundant in minerals and micro-nutrients essential for plant growth and vegetable and flower development. Read more on page 238.

3. Making your own compost is excellent for the environment: less waste curbside is a spectacular family goal, and composting is a great way to reduce your home's heavy yard and kitchen waste. Just think—if every home made an effort to compost as much as possible, tons and tons of heavy waste would no longer need to be hauled unnecessarily to landfill sites in diesel-spewing garbage trucks.

Add compost to your garden for richer results and fuller crops.

WHAT CAN BE ADDED TO A COMPOST PILE:

- Leaves
- Dry grass, lawn clippings and sod (chopped into small chunks)
- Hay, straw, pine needles or cedar (not too many pine or cedar needles, or they will change the pH (1–2 gal./5–10 L per month maximum)
- Annual weeds (before they go to seed)
- Lint from the dryer
- Garden clippings
- Houseplant debris
- Woodchips and sawdust
- Fireplace ash in thin layers
- Shredded newspaper
- Cardboard toilet-paper rolls
- Brown-paper shopping bags
- Cut flowers
- Human or pet hair
- Fruit or fruit waste including pits
- Tea in bags or loose leaf
- Coffee grounds and filters
- Eggshells and cardboard egg cartons
- Kitchen food scraps and peelings (with a few exceptions; see below)

Fallen leaves can be extremely detrimental to a lawn, smothering it and preventing light from penetrating, hindering its regular growth cycle.

WHAT CANNOT BE PLACED IN A COMPOST PILE:

- Pasta
- Fish or fish scraps
- Meat scraps or bones
- Fats or grease
- Dairy products
- Excessive grass clippings (mix moderate amounts with other materials)
- Diseased plants
- Annual weeds that have gone to seed
- Twigs over ½ in. (1 cm) thick
- Roots of perennial weeds
- Human or pet waste
- Treated wood
- Paint, chemicals, pesticides or herbicides
- Charcoal or coal ashes

Weeds are good material for the compost box; however, remove flowers or seed heads, as many seeds can survive the composting process to haunt your future garden shows.

I hear it is important to mix the compost box—how can I best do this?

A. Opposite to a good martini, your compost is better stirred, not shaken.

Stirring, mixing or churning the internal ingredients of a compost box is very important. If you've never done so, you might have noticed that the material from the base of the box is a very dense, heavy and wet black compost. This is not necessarily a bad thing for nourishing material for the garden, but it would definitely have to be mixed thoroughly with soil to be suitable to use.

A lighter material that wouldn't run the risk of being so heavy it could smother the roots of your plants would be better. This is particularly important if you plan to use compost for smaller plants, bulbs or vegetables.

Mixing your compost will also assist the process of decomposition by bringing some of the heavier bottom material to the top of the pile.

The result of your composting journey should be a relatively dark and light material, ready for use in your garden or to make compost tea.

There are three main reasons to mix your compost box regularly:

1. It will allow moisture to penetrate more easily, draining through the box quickly and preventing a poorly functioning compost box. If moisture does not penetrate, the contents won't be able to "heat up" and decompose.

2. It will mix earthworms evenly throughout the box. Worms feed on the waste and in turn break down the material that much faster.

3. It will also allow air to circulate more easily within the box, which is integral for a functional and healthy compost.

Mixing your compost box is difficult without a compost turner. I have tried it with a garden fork, but I was too restricted by the walls to dig deeply into the box. A compost turner is an aluminum shaft, about 4 ft. (120 cm) long, with a handle on one end and a heavy-duty butterfly on the other. When you push the compost turner into your box, the butterfly end folds up so that the shaft is easily inserted deep within the compost. Then when you pull it up, the butterfly opens and drags the base ingredients to the top. I recommend about 15 to 20 insertions to mix the box thoroughly every 8 to 10 weeks.

Q. *I've heard that making compost tea is easy and of great benefit to plants—how do I do this?*

A. Compost tea is definitely not something that you'd pour yourself a mug of, but plants absolutely love it.

Compost tea is the liquid derived from steeping compost in water. The end result looks like a dark tea and is rich in minerals, micro-nutrients and micro-organisms beneficial to plants. It puts healthy biology back into the earth, particularly for container-grown plants that have much of their nutritional elements washed out of the soil from constant summer watering.

That said, compost tea is not so much a fertilizer as a nutritional supplement, a powerhouse infusion that will improve plant health, crop quality and even resistance to disease.

This solution is best used in the garden after we've completed our spring planting, for pots of herbs or flowers, and for permanent container plantings where there is no room to add any more solid matter in and around the plants. Compost tea can also be used as a foliar spray, to help prevent disease and invigorate the plant leaves, so don't be afraid to water from the top of the plant and let it drip down to the roots.

Every plant can benefit from compost tea, so be generous and feed often. No cup and saucer required.

Here's how to brew a batch:

1. I'll assume you already have a compost box, as without it this process would be like making lemonade without lemons. You'll also require a 4-gal. (20-L) bucket, a shovel, cold water and a porous (cheesecloth-like) bag. You can also use a burlap sack, pantyhose, or even a recycled shopping bag, as many are made of a porous material and the handles could come in handy. There are many other options, but it must be a bag that will allow water to flow through while retaining the solid bits. An onion bag, for example, would be a little too porous.

2. Head over to the compost box and shovel approximately three medium-sized scoops of compost into your bag.

3. Place your bag into the bucket, open side up and add water, ensuring its level is below the top of the bag.

4. Slowly move the bag up and down about 10 times so that the water flows through the bag and the compost within it. You'll be surprised by how quickly the water will start to turn dark as the compost "steeps."

5. Take out the bag and you're left with about half a bucket of dark water.

Top up the bucket with fresh water and use this solution to water your plants.

You should remove compost from your box every six to eight months, depending on how much material you add to the box every week.

6. Repeat the above steps three times, using the same bag of compost. The third time, you might want to let it steep overnight to get a concoction as rich as the first two batches.

7. Finally, the remnants in the bag are useful as mulch in the garden.

Below: A layer of mulch between rows of celery and kale in this vegetable garden keeps weeds down and moisture in.

I recommend that you serve compost tea to your fruits, vegetables and even flowers once or twice a month. For example, a mature tomato plant would love about 4 cups (1 L) of compost tea each time you brew a batch. Watch your garden flourish with the natural and organic benefits of compost tea.

USING FERTILIZERS EFFECTIVELY

Q. *I want to use only organic fertilizer on my vegetables and herbs—would liquid seaweed on its own be enough?*

A. I'm a huge proponent of liquid seaweed for many reasons, including its potency as a fertilizer and its pest-control qualities.

There are hundreds of varieties of seaweed, all with different components and nutritional values. So much potential compost material, and it's often

available for the taking from lakes and oceans. But if you are going to forage for some seaweed, ensure you are in a public area that doesn't prohibit this and take detached pieces of seaweed only so that you're not ripping it out with the roots and disrupting an ecosystem.

Seaweed can be of huge benefit to the garden, particularly because it is an organic fertilizer rich in such micro-nutrients as boron, copper, iron, manganese, zinc and more—all key components for healthy crops and difficult to find in any other organic form. Keep in mind that seaweed is not a complete fertilizer, though, as it contains less than 1 percent of any of the major elements: nitrogen, phosphorus and potash. Therefore, supplementing with a balanced organic fertilizer will be required to offer complete nutritional fulfillment.

Seaweed also contains hormones that will stimulate plant growth—just one more terrific attribute of this ocean-derived fertilizer.

Personally (and scientifically) speaking, I suggest that spraying liquid seaweed on your plants is as important as watering the soil with it, because when it's sprayed onto leaves it's absorbed quickly and directly into the plant for stronger stem and leaf growth, earlier blossoming and more thorough fruit set. Not only that, but in controlled test gardens, seaweed-sprayed vegetables had anywhere from between 50 to nearly 200 percent more roots than plants not spritzed with it.

Whichever method you choose—foliar feeding through spraying on your plants, or mixing with water to apply to the soil, or both—please follow the instructions on the label, as different manufacturers offer unique blends and specific mixing recommendations.

If I want to feed my lawn with a granular fertilizer, what setting should I set my spreader at to ensure I use the correct amount? **Q.**

A. Every lawn fertilizer has a different coverage per kilogram rate, for various reasons but mostly because of the actual amount of fertilizer in the bag. That's right—just because you buy a bag of lawn fertilizer that is twice the size of any other for maybe half the price, it doesn't mean you're getting the best value for your money.

Often manufacturers will produce fertilizer types to hit a price point for the retailer. This is usually done by adding fillers. A low price point often means more filler, which then means the product will provide less coverage and only a portion of what is in the bag is actually nutrition.

Not that the fillers are bad for your lawn—it's just that there is not much value to them. Vermiculite and an inexpensive calcium carbonate are both fillers often used to increase the volume and/or weight of a bag.

Check the coverage carefully to ensure that you're getting a quality fertilizer.

As a general rule, a 22-lb. (10-kg) bag of lawn fertilizer should offer a minimum of approximately 4,000 sq. ft. (372 sq. m) of coverage.

So how can we figure out what setting to use on the fertilizer spreader? As far as I'm concerned, without more information, you truly can't. As it depends on both the density of the product and the size of the granule of fertilizer, it's nearly impossible to determine the exact setting for one of the many spreader models available. I do, however, have a solution. Yay!

Here's what I suggest:

1. Pace off your lawn and come up with an estimate of its area—an approximation is all that's required.

2. Review the coverage capacity of the product you have purchased to determine how much you need for your lawn size. Let's say that you have approximately 2,000 sq. ft. (186 sq. m) of lawn, and the bag of lawn fertilizer covers 4,000 sq. ft. (372 sq. m). In this case, you would put half the bag in the fertilizer hopper, which would be the appropriate amount to cover your lawn area.

3. Set the spreader on one of the lowest settings. Apply the fertilizer back and forth, until you've covered the entire lawn area; then, in a grid-like fashion, go back and forth in the other direction. Keep doing this until the hopper is empty. This will ensure the fertilizer is dispensed evenly and accurately over the entire lawn area.

A broadcast spreader (with the round barrel) is the best choice for applying granular fertilizers. It allows you to achieve an even distribution so that you don't end up with the dreaded stripes in your lawn!

Hydrangeas offer a big show in the shade, as their flower heads can reach up to 1 ft. (30 cm) across. Proven Winners photo

What soil amendments will keep my hydrangea blue?

Q.

A. There are so many hues of hydrangeas—from white to dark purple to just about every shade in between—and you can influence their colour somewhat with the chemical composition of the soil they are growing in.

First, your hydrangea has to be in good health. With a shallow root system, the hydrangea family is naturally susceptible to overheating and drying out. The biggest reason for this is that the hydrangea has an abundance of leaves that the root system must work hard to keep cooled. Every leaf will transpire, kinda like sweating, in the heat, and the plant's roots will need to replenish that moisture—assuming there's adequate water in the soil for the roots to draw from. Therefore, hydrangeas prefer a slightly shady area. I recommend an eastern exposure where the sun is gone by early afternoon or a filtered-light situation where the plant is shaded by other plants during the hottest part of the day.

Now that you have your hydrangea nicely settled in a cool spot, we can move on to how to affect the colour of your healthy plant:

White stays white

First of all, pretty much any white hydrangea will always be white. Yes, some varieties of white are whiter, others more beige, and some will change from white to antique white or very faded pink. You get the picture. The fact is they will always be "white" hydrangeas, as opposed to a more vibrant colour. You will not be able to change them from white to a bright pink or blue.

Choose a lighter colour of hydrangea, like pink, that will stand out more in a shady location.
Proven Winners photo

There are now probably thousands of hydrangea varieties that have been cultivated, but I'm going to refer to the most popular species by far: *Hydrangea macrophylla*, or what's commonly referred to as the mophead family. Yes, this does sound like a rock band from the sixties, but mophead refers to the big pompom-style flower heads typical to this family. The flower colour of this species is determined by the pH of the soil, which you can influence in these ways:

Blue: The lower the pH (or more acidic the soil), at least below 6 on the pH scale, the more blue or purple the flower will become. So to blue up blooms, add aluminum sulphate (available at your local garden centre) at a rate of about 1 lb. (500 g) per mature plant every spring and fall. Simply sprinkle it evenly on the soil around the entire plant, 2–4 ft. (60–120 cm) from its stems.

Pink: By contrast, the higher the pH (or more alkaline the soil), above 7 on the pH scale, the more pink the flower will be. So if you are partial to pink, add dolomite lime at a rate of about 2 lb. (1 kg) per mature plant every spring and fall in the same manner as the aluminum sulphate.

Understand, however, that neither aluminum sulphate nor lime will work as fast as, say, adding chocolate powder to milk. By adding either element, you are slowly shifting the pH of the soil to a preferred level that, over the course of a year, will influence the colour of your hydrangea blossoms. And to keep this colour, you will need to replenish your soil every year with aluminum sulphate or lime to maintain the desired pH level.

SOLUTIONS TO SOIL ISSUES

My soil is sandy—how can I fix it fast?

A. Sandy soil is not necessarily a bad thing, as shrubs, flowers and crops can easily root into it and grow a large, healthy root system. There are even some plants that prefer a sandy soil—for instance, the many drought-resistant plants available at your garden centre, and such Mediterranean herbs as rosemary, thyme and lavender, which need a well-draining, sandy location. But if you wish to improve your soil's moisture- and nutrition-retaining capabilities, you will need to mix in healthy amounts of such organic material as compost, coir and manure to a depth of approximately 1 ft. (30 cm). Garden areas with sandy soil are best mulched annually to insulate plants and prevent moisture from escaping quickly.

Q. *Will the addition of lime make my heavy, clay-based soil more suitable for gardening?*

A. Adding Dolomite lime at a rate of 44 lb. (20 kg) per 1,000 sq. ft. (93 sq. m) in spring and fall helps break down a clay-based material, but thoroughly mixing in organic material, such as compost, coir, sand and manure, will also be necessary.

Bark chips also work well to open up a clay-based soil (don't use cedar, though, as this can be toxic to plants), but as they use nitrogen in their decomposition process, you will need to provide a nitrogen-rich fertilizer to garden areas containing chips.

Breaking up or loosening and lightening a heavy clay is imperative for success with soft-rooted plants, such as vegetables or annuals.

Q. *My planters and the large ceramic pots on my patio dry out very quickly in the summer—how can I prevent this?*

A. Here are some tricks to prevent your planters from drying out so fast:

1. Start out with a large pot (18 in./45 cm in diameter or larger). This is vitally important, because one good drying out of your container will not only affect the health of your plants but could outright kill them. This is not to say that you can't have success in smaller containers, but you'll need to be able to devote the time and attention required for frequent watering, so they don't go dry.

Logically, the larger the container, the more soil it will hold, and the more soil, the more water-retention the planting will have. Soil is like a sponge—put a large water-filled sponge on a table next to a smaller one also soaked to capacity. I don't have to tell you which sponge is going to dry out faster.

The drying-out of soil is intensified in a container, as opposed to out in the garden, since isolated earth in a pot will heat up faster when exposed to sun and warm temperatures. A large container is important not only through summer but also for the winter months, helping to insulate and protect plants from cold that can penetrate through the sides as well as the soil's surface.

2. In addition to good-quality moisture-retentive soil, there are other ingredients you can add to help prevent the planting from drying out too quickly.

At your local garden centre, look for Soil Moist, a unique product that resembles sand when dry but swells into almost dime-sized cubes of what looks like clear gel when moistened. The granules retain their water-rich gel form until the soil starts to dry, then they gradually deplete themselves to release that moisture, only to return to the gel state once the planter is watered again.

Another soil additive for moisture retention is coco fibre, or coco coir, which is a by-product of coconut harvesting. This organic material is very fibrous and, mixed with soil, will help improve the drainage, prevent compaction (so that roots can grow easily and more freely through the soil) and, most importantly, hold nearly 10 times its weight in water. It decomposes slowly, lasting up to 5 years in the soil, so it is definitely a good investment that will prevent your plants from going to pot.

3. Mulching the top of planters with compost if there's room will also help to prevent soil from drying out too quickly.

4. Choose light-coloured patio containers, rather than dark brown or black, as darker colours absorb more heat than light shades, causing the soil to heat up and moisture to evaporate faster.

Left: A container filled with drought-tolerant succulents allows you to get away for a summer weekend escape without needing someone to come over and water the patio pets.
Right: With a little imagination, patio planters and containers have limitless options for style, colour and flavour.

MARVELLOUS MULCH AND MANURE

Q. *What is mulch, and why is it important?*

A. I looked up the word "mulch" in the dictionary, mostly because I was interested to see what the description would be in today's language: nowadays, the word "mulch" is used as an action as well as a noun. Here's what the dictionary had to say, and I have to admit, it made me chuckle:

"Strawy (which I don't believe is even a word) dung in a somewhat moist state, but not rotten, used for protecting newly planted shrubs and trees, etc. V.T. to cover with mulch."

"Strawy dung in a somewhat moist state" doesn't offer a great visual, but I'd have to say that I think the description the dictionary provides has not been updated in quite a few years…say, like 50! In today's gardening world, we refer to mulch as any material that a plant's roots can grow into, or that protects them from drying out or excessive cold. Soil, bark mulch, manure, compost, straw, leaves, grass clippings, coir or peat moss and even sawdust could be considered mulch.

We also use the word "mulch" as a verb, as in: "I should mulch my hydrangea." This refers to the action of placing mulch on the ground.

The biggest benefits of adding mulch are preventing shallow-rooted plants from drying out in the summer months and expanding the root system. A layer of mulch over the soil and roots of plants is going to act like a porous blanket that will slow the drawing of moisture and house an upward growth of the root system.

Gardeners also use mulch to suppress weed growth, or tidy the garden— as a layer of bark mulch can make an area look fresh and tidy, as well as cover weed seedlings or weed seeds to suppress them from growing.

What type of mulch you use doesn't make that much of a difference, other than to the way it might make your yard and garden look. Using straw mulch might have your yard appear like you're prepping for a horse show or cattle feeding, whereas a manure layer may have neighbours wondering "where's the beef?"

The other issue to consider is how the mulch's makeup might affect the established soil. For example, a mulch of mushroom manure will be a little more alkaline, whereas a mulch of tree bark is acidic and will use nitrogen as it decomposes.

THE SENSIBLE SOLUTION FOR SOIL-STARVED URBAN/SUBURBAN LANDSCAPES

As we discussed earlier (see page 232), because topsoil is usually stripped away from the landscapes of urban and suburban housing developments, much of our soil is in bad need of improvement. Although it would be overwhelming to dig all of the plants out to add a base of soil underneath, building up soil above ground is a sensible and highly doable solution.

Adding 1–3 in. (2.5–7.5 cm) of mulch over the root system of your plants will slowly build up a growing medium that the plants can grow roots into, which will help maintain their long-term health. I suggest applying mulch to a new landscape every spring for the first three years, and every second year thereafter, being careful not to smother a plant by placing the mulch too close to the trunk of a tree or stalk of a plant. A few inches away from the bark/stalk is all that's required.

Usually, my lost garden tools aren't this easy to find. Freshly laid mulch is bright, clean and helps suppress weed growth.

PLANT FALL RYE AS A LIVING MULCH

"Fall rye" is a rye grass generally grown as a "cover crop" over fallow soil. Gardeners and farmers use this living mulch as a means of preventing soil erosion, improving soil composition and adding organic nutrition primarily in areas where crops are grown.

During the fall—usually a month or so prior to the first frost— seed is scattered in empty beds where crops have been harvested, and the hay-like rye quickly germinates and grows to about 2 ft. (60 cm). It is a cool-weather crop, hardy to -4F/-20C.

At any point prior to its going to seed, usually a month or two before planting new crops for the year, the grassy rye can be rototilled or dug in, adding nourishment and organic material to the soil.

Q. *What is the best manure to add to my garden?*

A. Looks like I'm going to resort to talking crap in my book.

You know, though, this is an interesting question that many people have a surprisingly strong preference about. If I was to tell an avid chicken-manure lover to switch manures, I might as well give up now. And, really, if they're having success with a specific manure, then they should stick with it.

To tell you the truth, one type of manure isn't much different from the next. They all are composed mostly of organic material, which every plant will benefit from. So it doesn't really matter which one you choose—chicken (poultry), steer (cow), lamb or mushroom (horse). (Mushroom manure is not actually mushroom poop, which I'm surprised some people have assumed; mushrooms cannot actually offer any form of waste other than the little ends we cut off before cooking them. "Mushroom manure" is simply horse manure, on which mushroom growers raise their fungal crops.)

Now, like anyone else, I also have a preferred back-end waste to use in my garden and planters, and it just happens to be mushroom manure, for these reasons:

Mushroom manure is usually coarser, with a heavy hay component that will help aerate a vegetable garden when thoroughly mixed in.

250

1. Mushroom manure doesn't have the horrible smell that chicken manure has. Yikes—chicken manure can be intense. Personally, I'd rather not gag as I use manure in my garden and planters.

2. Mushroom manure is a little more alkaline than most kinds of manure, so it helps to marginally increase the pH level of the naturally acidic soil in my garden. Knowing the pH of your soil can come in handy, because if you live in a region with alkaline soil, then you wouldn't necessarily want to further increase the pH. For more on the pH level of your soil, see page 49.

3. Most importantly, my top reason for preferring mushroom manure is that it comes from horses, meaning that it has a high straw content, making it very porous. This will help break up a heavy soil, making it easier for roots to grow and for water to penetrate deeply.

Although all manure contains some nutritional elements, this is nominal when compared with its most important aspect—the organic material that it will add to your existing earth.

There is more than one use for a pile of bagged manure... what's that smell?

Index

....

Index

Harbour Publishing Co. Ltd.
P.O. Box 219, Madeira Park, BC, V0N 2H0
www.harbourpublishing.com

Cover photograph by Jay Shaw
Edited by Carol Pope
Index by Stephen Ullstrom
Cover design by Anna Comfort O'Keeffe
Text design by Roger Handling, Terra Firma Digital Arts
Printed on chlorine-free paper made with 10% post-consumer waste
Printed and bound in Canada

Canada Council
for the Arts
Conseil des Arts
du Canada

BRITISH COLUMBIA
ARTS COUNCIL
An agency of the Province of British Columbia

Harbour Publishing acknowledges financial support from the Government of Canada through the Canada Book Fund and the Canada Council for the Arts, and from the Province of British Columbia through the BC Arts Council and the Book Publishing Tax Credit.

Library and Archives Canada Cataloguing in Publication

Vander Zalm, Wim
    Just ask Wim! : down-to-earth gardening answers / Wim Vander Zalm.

Includes index.
ISBN 978-1-55017-587-5

    1. Gardening—British Columbia—Pacific Coast—Miscellanea.
I. Title.

SB450.97.V36 2013   635   C2013-900199-9